Changing Kids' Games

Second Edition

G.S. Don Morris, PhD
California State Polytechnic University

Jim Stiehl, PhD
University of Northern Colorado

Human Kinetics

Library of Congress Cataloging-in-Publication Data

Morris, G.S. Don.
    Changing kids' games / by G.S. Don Morris, Jim Stiehl. -- 2nd ed.
      p. cm.
    Includes bibliographical references (p.   ).
    ISBN 0-88011-691-9
    1. Physical education for children. 2. Games. 3. Movement
education. 4. Sports for children. I. Stiehl, Jim. II. Title.
    GV443.M66   1999   98-27142
    372.1'337--dc21   CIP

ISBN: 0-88011-691-9

Copyright © 1989, 1999 by Gordon S. Morris and Jim Stiehl

Figure 4.2 on page 59 is reprinted with permission from the *Journal of Physical Education, Recreation & Dance*, April, 1990, pages 23-27. *JOPERD* is a publication of the American Alliance for Health, Physical Education, Recreation and Dance, 1900 Association Drive, Reston, VA 20191.

Acquisitions Editor: Scott Wikgren; **Developmental Editor:** Elaine Mustain; **Assistant Editors:** Melinda Graham, Phil Natividad, Melissa Feld; **Copyeditor:** Bonnie Pettifor; **Proofreader:** Sue Fetters; **Graphic Designer:** Nancy Rasmus; **Graphic Artist:** Yvonne Winsor; **Photo Editor:** Boyd LaFoon; **Cover Designer**: Jack Davis; **Photographer (cover):** Tom Roberts; **Photographer (interior):** Tom Roberts; **Illustrators:** Patrick Griffin, Tom Roberts; **Printer:** Versa Press

Printed in the United States of America   10 9 8 7 6 5 4 3 2 1

Human Kinetics
Web site: http://www.humankinetics.com/

United States: Human Kinetics
P.O. Box 5076
Champaign, IL 61825-5076
1-800-747-4457
e-mail: humank@hkusa.com

Canada: Human Kinetics
475 Devonshire Road Unit 100
Windsor, ON N8Y 2L5
1-800-465-7301 (in Canada only)
e-mail: humank@hkcanada.com

Europe: Human Kinetics, P.O. Box IW14
Leeds LS16 6TR, United Kingdom
(44) 1132 781708
e-mail: humank@hkeurope.com

Australia: Human Kinetics
57A Price Avenue
Lower Mitcham, South Australia 5062
(088) 277 1555
e-mail: humank@hkaustralia.com

New Zealand: Human Kinetics
P.O. Box 105-231, Auckland 1
(09) 523 3462
e-mail: humank@hknewz.com

To Muska, our mentor since 1964,
who ensured that after each meeting
we would not leave with more of himself,
but with more of ourselves

Contents

Preface

A simple idea with simple beginnings. That is how we would characterize this book. But although the idea may be simple, little did we realize 20 years ago the profound impact that changing games can have in the hands of a committed teacher. Take Robin, for instance, who was disgruntled with a traditional game that was involving too few players. She took a risk by inviting the players to begin changing various aspects of the game. Soon thereafter the game had become everyone's favorite. Those with and without disabilities alike played the game, even at recess and after school. Students enthusiastically welcomed homework ("homefun!") pertaining to the game, created a website for sharing with and inviting new games from others, and designed their own games book as a project with their classroom teacher. Physical education has become unified with the rest of the school's curriculum, and Robin credits these accomplishments to her willingness to risk changing the status quo.

In the ten years since publication of the first edition of this book, many activities in physical education programs have been soundly criticized. In our continued attempt to remedy this situation, our charge in this edition remains the same; that is, with proper motivation and ingenuity, any teacher can develop games and activities appropriate to all players in a single setting. We remain sensitive and responsive to the child who has the most to gain from physical activity, yet at the same time is the most easily discouraged. Too often the discouragement stems, at least in part, from activities that are not designed with the student's best interests in mind.

Our framework for changing and creating games is fundamentally the same as in the previous edition: understand the basic structure of all games, then modify that structure to alter and invent games that suit the needs and interests of everyone involved. Naturally, however, we took this opportunity to update *Changing Kids' Games* in this second edition. We have retained information from the first edition that our readers have told us has been most useful and included some new material. Specifically, in a new chapter entitled "Understanding Games Teaching" (chapter 4), we have asked Kevin Taylor to outline this increasingly popular "Games for Understanding" ("GFU") approach to games presentation. We have also removed some of the less used games and added several new ones.

Part I, "How to Alter and Invent Games," begins with a look at why games are played and why we think games are important. Chapter 2 outlines simplified step-by-step procedures for modifying games, and chapter 3 introduces strategies for involving others in games-changing efforts. As mentioned, chapter 4 discusses in detail the Games for Understanding (or tactical) method of teaching sports. It includes detailed examples from both soccer and badminton, showing how to devise simple games that teach the skills involved in the more complex games.

Part II, "Examples of Game Changes," offers an assortment of games and possible variations of those games. We've included numerous new games, categorizing all games differently than in the first edition: "Adventure Games" (chapter 5), "Academic Games" (chapter 6), "International Games" (chapter 7), and "Old Favorites . . . and More" (chapter 8). This new organizational strategy reflects practices in the field and responds to suggestions from readers over the last nine years.

This book, however, is not simply a compilation of activities, such as cultural games, teamwork ideas, and the like. Rather, it provides a method for modifying or creating any activity to better suit your purposes, resources, and players. *Changing Kids' Games, 2nd Edition*, will allow you to rely less on other books and more on your own ability to respond to your own students' needs. In other words, we give you more than 40 games *and* the means for creating 40,000 more. These are simple ideas with profound implications, making this volume a thinking person's game book.

Acknowledgments

As in the previous edition, we are grateful to a number of colleagues for their assistance. Kevin Taylor, PhD, was particularly helpful in this regard. He authored chapter 4 on the Games for Understanding approach. Reid Cross provided suggestions and direction for several of the adventure games—and tried them all (rain or shine). Scott Wikgren of Human Kinetics has offered support and encouragement since we first approached him 12 years ago and then directed us to this edition's developmental editor, Elaine Mustain, whose patient prodding ensured that we said what we meant and meant what we said.

Finally, we both wish to acknowledge the "genius" behind this work, Peter Morris (no longer a pint-size runt); Kari Morris (proof that daughters are a blessing); and Jim's partner, Julie (she can touch anyone with her uplifting smile).

Part I How to Alter and Invent Games

This section of the book provides you with strategies for adapting known games and creating new ones. We show you how to use a wide range of materials and equipment to develop games that are appropriate for all ages and abilities, in all kinds of places, and under a variety of circumstances. Indeed, although we have written this book primarily for games leaders working with young people, the concepts apply to players of all ages. In short, you're not likely to find your favorite "already-designed" game here; instead, you'll learn how to create new favorites of your own design.

Experience has taught us that games leaders need not be familiar with a large number of games. Rather, we have found that many players thoroughly enjoy games they know well, preferring to play them again and again, instead of learning new ones. We have also found that many games described in various books are not within the capabilities of all players and thus may require modification anyway. Consequently, we encourage you to use this section of the book to help you take the liberty of changing games that are familiar to you as well as invent new games especially suited to your purposes and players.

In the first chapter, we explore the nature of games and some possibilities available through games. In the ensuing chapters we offer a model for understanding the structure of all games, specific strategies for creating games, and suggestions for instructing and encouraging others to alter and invent games. As you read through these chapters, keep in mind that the games you and your players design will be limited only by your imaginations.

Chapter 1

Why Play Games?

Over the years, many people, from close friends and colleagues to distant acquaintances, have asked us, "What is changing kids' games all about?" Before we can answer this question, we must first clear up some misconceptions.

For starters, this book is not a list of games organized according to some scheme. The literature is replete with games categorized by play space (e.g., playgrounds, gyms, turf and lawn, water, city streets); by playthings (e.g., balls, racquets, baskets, hula hoops, ropes); by players (e.g., singles, doubles, group, mass); by purposes (e.g., running, dancing, cooperation, skill development, endurance); and by a host of other classification schemes. Frequently, too, the games are accompanied by game descriptions, "Bright Ideas," surveys, proven teacher tips, and "If you are tired of the same old stuff and if you order today, you'll receive a bonus 25 new, powerful, teacher-tested games."

Nor are we trying to justify or validate any certain point of view regarding the use and worth of games. Granted, we will discuss a few reasons why people might use and participate in games, but we are not advocating that you put games to any particular use. And finally, we will neither explain how to incorporate games into a program, nor suggest ways to present and use games. These issues are best discussed by proponents of specific approaches (e.g., Project Adventure's incorporation of fantasy into games or Peter Werner and others' descriptions of a Games for Understanding approach).

Certainly, games workshops and games books are useful resources for amassing a collection of games. Yet, with the strategies we'll suggest in this book, you will be able to successfully design a virtually unlimited number of your own games to best suit your individual needs and resources. So, rather than presenting games *per se* or justifications of games or explaining how and why to implement games, we will teach you how to modify and invent games for *your* purposes.

Our Basic Premises

Anytime we adopt, adapt, or invent a game, we do so with the following in mind:

- Games are not sacred; kids are. If a game is not appropriate for even a single player, it is worth examining and altering to accommodate that player.
- Games are for everyone, but not all games—at least not in their "traditional" configurations. To illustrate, in its current form, professional baseball might be ideal for some players. Few would argue, however, that professional rules, equipment, and expectations are appropriate for third graders. Instead, to accommodate this group, substantial alterations are necessary.
- You *can* modify any game to include anyone, obliging a wide spectrum of abilities, interests, needs, and resources.

Some Basic Choices

Whenever we play games, at least three choices present themselves: keep 'em, dump 'em, or change 'em; and whichever choices we make carry certain implications.

Figure 1.1   You can modify any game to include anyone.

Keep 'Em

The first choice, to keep 'em—continue playing games in their current form—often disregards our first principle; that is, games are not sacred, kids are. We frequently see teachers using a game that clearly does not suit some of the players' needs, yet the game continues under the rationale of, say, tradition. "Kickball," we've been told, "is a tried and true game for elementary-age children. If it was good enough for their parents, it's good enough for them."

In addition to the tradition rationale, we also encounter the cart-before-the-horse mentality. In this mode of operation, a games leader selects and runs a game with little attention to why it might be useful or not. A justification emerges only when we press the games leader for one. Again using kickball as an example, we hear claims that kickball promotes running, throwing, catching, and kicking skills. This might be a reasonable argument were it not for the fact that the players having the greatest need to improve these skills (e.g., the physically awkward child) often have the fewest opportunities to do so. Instead, the child with poor catching and throwing skills languishes in deep right field. And the one lacking in kicking and running proficiency is not likely to be the leadoff kicker, the player who has the greatest number of times at the plate. In other words, those with the greatest needs are frequently the same ones who are relegated to less challenging roles and who become most easily discouraged. So the justification seems more an afterthought than anything else.

Dump 'Em

A second choice is to dump 'em; that is, eliminate games that are unsuitable in their present form. A recent practice by some has been to assign certain games to the "Physical Education Hall of Shame," a repository for games considered inappropriate for today's curriculum. To us, this amounts to throwing out the baby with the bathwater. Years ago when Duck, Duck, Goose became a scapegoat for games deemed developmentally inappropriate, we suggested that it might be worthwhile to reconsider this and other "problem" activities. Our proposal was to examine aspects of an activity that make it "inappropriate," then look for characteristics that might be worth keeping, even accentuating. With Duck, Duck, Goose, lack of active participation and singling out an individual for failure are good reasons to frown on the activity. However, the thrill of suspense and the joy and skills of chasing and fleeing are aspects worth preserving and enhancing. This type of thinking led us to a third choice: change 'em.

Change 'Em

As noted in the preface to our first edition of this book, we adopted our "change 'em" perspective about 30 years ago. During the summer of 1970, Don's son, Peter, informed us that in order to play together, our game would require some adjustments:

It is no secret. The ideas in this book originated not from lofty adult visions or abstractions, but from the tearful complaints of a little boy whose daddy and "uncle" were not including him in a backyard game of croquet. This pint-sized, cat-chasing whirlwind of noise and dust was not going to allow two adults to lock him out. Indeed, the adults were astonished by his persistence, as well as by his cleverness at "distorting" the game so all could play (Morris & Stiehl, 1989, p. xi).

From that moment on, we were both committed to including all players, regardless of ability, age, or experience. Hence, the beginning of a perspective that we have advocated since before the first printing of *How to Change the Games Children Play* (Morris, 1976) and *Elementary Physical Education: Toward Inclusion* (Morris, 1980). We also recognized that a critical resource would be the players themselves. Their ingenuity, imagination, and natural inclination toward playing games became a major source of inspiration and vitality.

In essence, our change 'em approach identifies features that are common to all games (e.g., players, movements, limits) and then alters certain aspects of those features to change an existing game or create a new one. For some, the mechanics of changing a game are much simpler than overcoming or bypassing the mental blocks that can inhibit us from doing so. New ideas and change are sometimes less comfortable than routines and tradition. But routines can "imprison your thinking" and it may be worthwhile to "assault your assumptions . . . and to give yourself 'a whack on the side of the head'" (Bushnell, 1983, p. xv). Although more challenging, the change 'em (versus keep 'em or dump 'em) approach seems to be the most sensible one if you want activities that will fit your purposes, values, teaching styles, resources, and, of course, your players.

Games: Since Days of Yore

Games are popular not only in schools and recreation programs but also in society at large. If you look at our bookshelves (e.g., *Ancient Olympic Games, Bargaining Games: The Art of Negotiation, Basic Computer Games, Fun and Games in Marriage*), our films and television shows (e.g., *Singled Out, The New Dating Game, Lovelines, Bzzz*), and our language (e.g., "Don't play games with me!" and "What's your game, anyway?"), you might conclude that people are preoccupied with games.

We can trace human interest in games back thousands of years. For example, tic-tac-toe was, for many of us, our first introduction to board games. But archeologists suggest that games involving filling grid spaces alternately with Xs and Os have been played by humans as long as they have been able to take a stick in hand and scratch a line in the dirt. In fact, a diagram for tic-tac-toe was found cut into the roofing slabs of an ancient Egyptian temple built in the 14th century B.C. Archeologists speculate that

Figure 1.2 Human interest in games can be traced back thousands of years.

they are relics of some game-playing stonemasons who relaxed with a game of tic-tac-toe during lunch. Subsequent versions of this game have been found in Roman ruins and medieval cathedrals, but the offshoots were not always considered child's play. Some frowned upon variations of tic-tac-toe as dangerous holdovers from pagan rites; periodically, they were even banned.

As another example, rolling an object to hit another object is a game as old as Western civilization. Middle Eastern cultures have played versions of it for thousands of years, the Greeks viewed such games as excellent exercise, and the Romans spread them throughout ancient Europe. Finally, earlier combined forms of badminton and soccer were played in the Far East more than 2000 years ago when young Oriental cadets kicked a small feathered ball to hone their agility, while shopkeepers kicked the ball in the streets to keep warm on slow winter days. A more recent hunt-and-capture game, chess, was a product of the Middle Ages and still enjoys considerable popularity. A type of football, mentioned long ago by Shakespeare in two of his plays, was banned by Edward II and other medieval kings because of danger to life and limb, but a variation of the game remains popular today as rugby. The spelling bee, a favorite during the last century, is still with us today. And Parker Brothers' Monopoly, created in the 1930s, continues as one of our most popular board games. Indeed, the books written on the historical, scientific, and educational aspects of play and games are numerous, demanding a distinct scholarship of their own. Suffice it to say, then, that people have long appreciated games, and games have captured the imagination of adults and children alike.

Games: Fun, and Much More

When discussing games, it is useful to also examine the closely related concept of play. It has been said, however, that understanding the atom bomb is child's play compared to understanding child's play. Certainly, many scholars with diverse viewpoints have sought to understand the nature of play (Eisen, 1988), and finding any major point of agreement among all of them is difficult. Nonetheless, to provide a frame of reference, we must define *play*, and then *games*.

First, children seem to define themselves and their world through play. Consult any dictionary, and you will find many definitions of the word *play*. We regard play as an enjoyable, serious, voluntary activity that participants consider to be apart from the external world. Play is enjoyable because it is engaged in for "fun's sake," with little thought about its usefulness. Yet play is serious because it provides opportunities for enhancing a child's feelings of mastery and promoting his or her sense of being important. Play is unreal because players step out of reality, entering an imaginary world. Eating, writing a novel, and riding a motorcycle can be fun, serious, and voluntary, but they are not play because they are not apart from the real world. People play to lose themselves; paradoxically, however, people sometimes find themselves through play.

Unlike play, games are usually structured and have more or less predictable outcomes. Participants play games with a certain goal in mind; they do not have the complete freedom to follow impulses and are more confined because behavior becomes subordinated to the anticipated goals. In games, players place limitations on the play world and turn play into a contest. The limitations include prescribed space and time boundaries, agreed upon rules, and clearly defined goals. People play games with much energy and involvement; the more intense and serious the game-playing, the more likely the rewards of success and enjoyment. We can define *games*, then, as "activities confined by implicit rules, in which there is a contest between players in order to produce predictable outcomes." In short, a game is a voluntary contest with agreed upon rules and clearly defined goals.

Though many may consider games to be contests, the important differences between games and other contests (such as professional sports, war, and some human relationships) are that

- games, like other forms of play, step out of the "real" world;
- winning or losing is a short-lived condition relevant only to the game itself;
- games may be replayed with the same opponents; and
- games require cooperation by players in adhering to explicit rules and implicit game play behaviors, in other words, "fair" play.

Figure 1.3 In games, players place limitations on the play world and turn play into a contest.

What Can Games Do?

Most teachers, coaches, recreation leaders, and parents want to contribute to the quality of young people's lives—their development, achievements, and overall well-being. One way of accomplishing this is through games. There is not universal agreement, however, on the value of games. Historically, many have disdained games as trivial and unimportant. Games are fun; hence, the reasoning goes, they are not legitimate activities, especially in schools. By way of contrast, some sports and other physical activities have long been praised as sources of character building, delinquency reduction, and leadership development. Only recently have educators begun to recognize games as important tools for improving instruction.

We suggest that the value of a game lies in the purpose for which it is designed. Some games may be designed solely for their enjoyment. Others may have more serious purposes, such as fostering certain attitudes and values, presenting academic subject matter, promoting socially desirable behaviors, enhancing physical skills, or encouraging the development of personal attributes such as honesty, bravery, perseverance, and acceptance of self and others. Still, a most important feature of game-playing is that participants enjoy themselves more when they are playing than when they are not. In short, whatever is acquired during game-playing is acquired with pleasure.

Why Movement Games?

There are games of chance, strategy, and physical skill, academic games, board games, party games—and even funeral games! In this book, we emphasize games involving movement. That is not to say that each game will have movement as its primary focus. For many of the games we will describe, movement is incorporated solely as a motivator. For other games in this book, movement itself is the primary ingredient. No matter what role movement plays in a particular game, however, all our games offer the players an opportunity to move.

Why? By its very nature, movement is powerful. It invites possibilities not readily available through other means (e.g., reading, watching movies, listening to tapes). First, movement can be fun, thereby adding to the enjoyment of games. Games are fun; movement games are doubly fun. Most importantly, however, movement comes naturally to kids, opening an exciting possibility: Through movement games we can contribute to the development of children and, at the same time, rest assured that they are enjoying themselves.

Indeed, activities involving movement afford unique opportunities and experiences. Through movement, for example, children can increase cardio-vascular efficiency and the range and effectiveness of motion. They can also release tension, gain personal understanding, test prowess, learn team-work, and simply derive pleasure from movement experiences. Thus, while children are learning movement games, they are improving themselves without recognizing it.

The fifth grade students at Adamsville School had been modifying games for quite some time when Lenny first arrived. One day, they happened to be playing a variation of kickball. Lenny had never played kickball. In fact, he had not played many games because most people agreed that a boy confined to a wheelchair could not participate in vigorous activities.

But this was a special class. The children immediately began to introduce themselves to Lenny and invited him to participate in the game. Lenny was frightened; he had been alone before—but never in this sense. This time he was alone in his belief that he could not participate in such a game. The other children were already embracing a "can-do" spirit and were determined to include this newcomer.

Lenny was assigned to the team at bat, some members of which had been deciding on a strategy for including him in a manner commensurate with his abilities. Instead of kicking a ball and running bases, Lenny had to maneuver his wheelchair through some obstacles and then squirt a water pistol at a paper cup that was balanced on a traffic cone. If he could get to the cup, knock it over, and return home without colliding with any of the obstacles, he was pronounced "safe."

Sometimes he succeeded, and sometimes he did not. He and his classmates determined what he *could* do, verified their strategy with us, and then agreed that this was an acceptable option. Lenny was no longer merely a spectator. His was not a case of token involvement, but of genuine participation—of inclusion.

Although we can easily justify movement and movement games from an academic standpoint, children (and adults) also benefit from the more personal, emotionally appealing aspects of movement games. For example, one pleasant recollection is the joy of watching a group of kindergartners trying to balance on roller skates for the first time, their brows creased with concentration, their eyes alight with excitement. What fun it is to teach these little people, people to whom movement games are a world of entertainment as well as a learning experience! Or the fifth grader who had been isolated for most of her life because of her spina bifida, invited to play in a modified soccer game—and proved to be the star of the day. Rather than defend the goal and attempt to prevent opposing players from scoring, she held a hula hoop through which her teammates would kick the ball to score points. That single event provided important breakthroughs in this child's self-confidence, skill development, and willingness to develop friendships. It also served to remind us of the potential value of movement games.

You can use games to assist any child in reaching his or her maximum cognitive, social, emotional, and physical potentials. Indeed, the unique contribution movement games can make to each child's development justifies their use. Although there is no consensus on the nature and priority of game purposes, the following sections list that which typifies what many people expect as they design and use games. You need select none of these goals at the expense of another.

Enhance Movement Skill Development

Any popular game or sport requires movement skill. The skills may be complex or relatively simple or basic. To enjoy a variety of activities, children must learn basic skills such as running, jumping, turning, kicking, and throwing. As they develop a repertoire of basic skills, they establish the

Figure 1.4 Movement games open exciting possibilities for everyone.

efficiency, ability, and versatility necessary for playing and enjoying many of the activities valued in our culture. This is important not only during the school years but also as the individual pursues leisure experiences later in life. The emergence of many movement skills is to some extent a matter of growth and development; but encouragement and instruction through movement games may be helpful if the child is to acquire or become proficient at more complicated skills.

Nurture Feelings of Self-Worth

By providing successful and meaningful movement game experiences, we can contribute to a child's healthy attitude toward self and others. Research suggests that a child's self-image and confidence depend in part on how skilled he or she is at certain games and activities (Harter & Robinson, 1993; Weiss et al., 1990). In addition to promoting skill development, we can give children time and opportunity to be thoughtful about themselves and their relationships with others. We can encourage them to express how they feel and develop empathy for others. Children who can accept themselves and their physical capabilities are more likely to participate willingly and enthusiastically in sports and other physical activities. They are also more likely to have positive relationships with their teachers, coaches, parents, and peers.

Promote Physical Fitness

As you probably well know, research clearly shows that many physical and psychological diseases affecting adults stem from inactivity. For example, conditions such as high blood pressure, coronary heart disease, and obesity can be partially attributed to a sedentary lifestyle. On the positive side, dynamic vitality, productivity, and health in our adult population are commonly associated with youth fitness. And simply put, fit children are more likely to grow into fit and healthy adults. Thus, we have a unique opportunity through movement games to contribute to children's strength, power, flexibility, postural alignment, endurance, and body composition. So, of course, these games should include all children, as children of all ability levels can reap fitness benefits.

Foster Enjoyment and Satisfaction

As previously mentioned, a prime ingredient in all movement games is enjoyment. Children enjoy participating in physical activity and find it personally satisfying. "Enjoyment," as used here, means more than simply "fun," however. To illustrate, a person may enjoy reading, painting, or perhaps training for a marathon. In the latter two examples, enjoyment involves discipline and hard work; consequently, it results in personal fulfillment and an ongoing pursuit of excellence, especially if the activity continues to be challenging. Likewise, in movement games, we can foster personal satisfaction, enrichment, and a sense of "aliveness" through activities that are enjoyable and motivating. Moreover, through games, we can nourish the child's active, playful spirit—surely a legitimate pursuit.

Figure 1.5   Children can learn how to learn, not simply how to perform as in this game of TP Shuffle (see chapter 5).

Invite Use of Cognitive Skills

Children can learn how to learn, not simply how to perform. Through movement games and certain deliberate ways of presenting these games, children may participate in specific cognitive operations, such as comparing and contrasting, categorizing, hypothesizing, inventing, synthesizing, making decisions, identifying and solving problems, thinking abstractly, and so on. The ability to think for oneself contributes to an individual's self-reliance and confidence as well as to his or her capacity to treat others with dignity and compassion.

Encourage a Sense of Community

A sense of belonging or interdependence is important in creating an optimal games climate. When children feel connected to and validated by others, that is, when they feel included as an integral part of a game, exciting opportunities unfold. First, when kids consider an atmosphere "safe," they are more willing to take risks—not irresponsible risk—but "dignified daring." And often that daring will lead to increased spontaneity, confidence, or determination. Second, a sense of belonging leads to intimate sharing with others and can help a shy, uncomfortable child become more open and willing to encourage and comfort others.

Concluding Remarks

As you can see, movement games offer a wealth of possibilities. They carry their own built-in motivation and can be particularly valuable for certain children, the reluctant learner, for instance, or the child in need of remedial help. Moreover, the fearful or rebellious, the bored or less-able children often play enthusiastically in a game, which then serves as a powerful incentive for learning and further participation. Certainly, these days, few of us doubt the usefulness of games. What concerns us is developing suitable games for our purposes. This, then, is the subject of the next chapter.

Chapter 2

How to Change Any Game

In some fashion, games are a part of every child's life. Whether you look indoors or outdoors, in winter or summer, in the city or country, on the seashore, in woodlands, or in the snow, you can usually find children who are playing games. They play in their backyards, on school grounds, and in parks, vacant lots, gymnasiums, and streets. The games they play are often derived from many sources from various countries. Some are common, thoroughly tried, traditional games. Others are variations of popular games. Still others are quite novel. Some require fairly standardized equipment; others make use of stones, pebbles, old T-shirts, holes in the sand, and diagrams drawn on the ground. In turn, we adults formalize many of these games and offer them to children, usually with some purpose—either stated or implicit—in mind.

The need hundreds of children's games leaders have expressed to us more often than any other is for games that accomplish some stated goal while still including all participants. The idea of modifying games to accomplish specific purposes generates many questions, however. Some of the questions that teachers, recreation specialists, and youth sports leaders have posed include the following:

- Can we use some of these ideas so we can conduct daily practices more efficiently?
- Can we design lead-up games more appropriately?
- How can we use these concepts to increase practice time and reduce waiting time?
- Do children's soccer fields and other playing areas need to duplicate adult playing areas (e.g., size, boundaries, and shape of field or court; size and location of goals, baskets, and so on)? The same question pertains to children's equipment.

Figure 2.1 How can we use these concepts to increase practice time and reduce waiting time?

- Is it feasible for leaders of youth sport programs to consider changing established and accepted sports to include more children, perhaps by matching the activity to the participants' developmental status, thereby enticing more of them to participate?
- Should the primary limitation in any game be the creativity and enthusiasm of its participants?

We will address many of these questions while demonstrating how *you* can design games that will achieve *your* purposes—while including every participant. Effective games provide congruity between purposes (what we intend to accomplish) and players (e.g., their skill levels, interests, and needs). When asking, "What do I intend to accomplish, and what characterizes my players?" your primary consideration should be whether a game's structure and demands will allow for purpose-player congruity. In other words, you must understand your purposes and your players before you can create a game that accommodates both.

Designing appropriate games requires three steps:

1. Understanding the basic structure of all games
2. Modifying a game's basic structure
3. Managing the game's degree of challenge or difficulty

We have adapted this procedure from a more detailed one (Morris & Stiehl, 1985) designed to match the nature of any participant (e.g., low-skilled, high-skilled, with or without disabilities) to any movement activity (e.g., dance, gymnastics, swimming, running).

Step One: Understanding the Basic Structure of All Games

When selecting, altering, or creating games to satisfy the demand for purpose-player congruity, you must make decisions about various aspects of games. For example, how many players will be involved, and what are their assignments and duties? What is the object of the game? How will you score it? What equipment is necessary? What is the layout of the playing area? Are there officials? Rules? Restrictions? The questions seem endless.

If we categorize game components according to some logical scheme, we can attack the game-changing puzzle one problem at a time.

We will present only one of many possible ways to cluster the decisions a games leader must address when designing games. Though there are other possibilities, we have successfully used the model offered here for almost 30 years. And although other authors have since used or slightly varied this basic model (e.g., Kirchner, 1992; Graham, Holt/Hale & Parker, 1993; Pangrazi & Dauer, 1995; Rohnke & Butler, 1995), we recently discovered a book published in 1930 entitled *Play Games!* by Albert Wegener. Wegener presents a fascinating array of "all the factors that are involved in various kinds of play. If these factors are arranged in columns, then by reading across or zigzag, endless combinations invent themselves; it is so mechanical that little thought is needed. . . . There are limitless possibilities, not all desirable it is true, but enough of them sufficiently useful to furnish a play leader all that he will ever need" (p. 9). In our much-simplified model, we suggest several major game categories, each of which can be subdivided into game components. As depicted in table 2.1, the categories and their components constitute the bricks and mortar of any game.

As we present the model in greater detail, keep in mind that although the categories and components are useful, you may develop a scheme more suitable for your own use.

Purposes

Paying attention to the first two categories, purposes and players, is critical if we are to ensure purpose-player congruity. Purposes can range from very simple, such as "to be active," to more complex, such as "to improve concentration; to promote thoughtfulness of others; to perform successfully a variety of gross body coordination and balance tasks; or to develop strength and cardiovascular endurance." In a single game, you may wish to

Table 2.1 Games Design Model

Purposes	Players	Movement
Develop motor skills	Individuals	Types
Enhance self-worth	Groups	Location
Improve fitness	Numbers	Quality
Enjoyment		Relationships
Satisfaction		Quantity
Develop cognitive skills		Sequence
Objects	**Organization**	**Limits**
Types and uses	Types	Performance
Quantity	Location	Environment
Location	Quantity	

promote a single purpose, or many. To avoid frustration, however, we suggest not trying to accomplish too many things at once. Instead, it helps to sequence your purposes and present them over a defined period of time (more about this process in the following chapter).

The game must facilitate at least one purpose. Purposes include the following, among many:

- To develop motor skills
- To promote self-worth
- To increase fitness
- To provide enjoyment and satisfaction
- To teach cognitive skills

We can then subdivide each of these purposes. For example, we might dissect cognitive skills according to a taxonomy of cognitive processing or thinking levels as outlined in 1956 by Bloom:

- Acquiring knowledge
- Comprehending, for example: interpreting, translating

- Applying knowledge to a variety of situations
- Analyzing, for example: identifying key relationships
- Synthesizing, for example: arranging an entire structure
- Evaluating, that is, making judgments

These are by no means the only, or the "best," goals to use when designing games, though. For instance, Hoffman, Young, and Klesius (1981), who work extensively with elementary-age children in physical education settings, might use the following objectives:

- Becoming aware
- Becoming independent
- Accepting and expressing feelings and ideas
- Accepting responsibilities and acting cooperatively
- Improving quality of responses
- Drawing relationships

Terry Orlick (1978), long involved with the cooperative games movement, might suggest cooperation, acceptance, involvement, and fun as the most important purposes of games.

As you can see, we are not attempting to promote one set of purposes over another. So just as we have settled upon purposes that suit our personal beliefs and intentions, feel free to select those you find suitable. But regardless of what purposes you choose, it is important to establish them clearly. Goals bring into focus what you are trying to accomplish, giving direction to you and your players.

Players

All games have players, but the number of players, their abilities, and other characteristics differ from game to game. Table 2.2 defines some of the decisions you might make regarding players.

Table 2.2 Players Component of the Games Design Model

Individual characteristics	Group characteristics	Numbers
Skilled or unskilled	Equal or unequal skills	Individuals
Male or female	Same sex or coed	Groups
Does or does not have a disability	Heterogeneous or homogeneous	Individuals per group

Initially you must decide whom you'll include in the game, and then to what extent and in what manner. Perhaps only very young children, children with disabilities, or only highly skilled players will participate; or perhaps you will combine ages, skill levels, or children with disabilities with those without disabilities. By attending to meaningful player characteristics, you can begin to define the types of games that may be most attractive and relevant to the players involved. For instance, it may be helpful to know whether a player is skilled or unskilled or that one child has poor self-esteem, another has a strong need to win, and yet another needs considerable assistance with basic movement skills. It may also help to know whether a child is visually impaired, or gifted, has asthma, enjoys baseball, and so on.

Thus, an important question to ask yourself is, "Am I attending to meaningful and useful player characteristics?" There is no clear-cut answer to this question, of course. But it is imperative that, in light of the game's purpose, you consider individual player characteristics carefully.

Along with individual player characteristics, you should decide which group characteristics are important. Since most games involve interactions among several players, consider the group's composition and how that may affect the design of a game. Will the group consist of various skill levels? Children small in stature? A wide age range? Mostly girls? As with individual players, you can classify a group along many dimensions. And again, the question is basically, "How useful is that classification scheme?"

Some group classifications are more likely than others to influence the nature of a game. You may, for example, group players according to physical

Figure 2.2 Consider the group's composition and how that may affect the design of a game.

size, age, ability, first letter of their last names, or color of clothes. Obviously some of these grouping strategies can affect a game substantially, whereas others may have little or no effect.

Lastly, you need to make some quantity decisions about players. How many individuals will play? How many at one time? Will there be more than one group and, if so, how many and of what size each? Will group sizes be equal or unequal? It's likely by this point that you have noticed that decisions about players relate closely to the purpose of the game as well as to considerations such as playing area size and equipment availability.

In some cases the decisions will be yours, while at other times the decisions may already have been made for you by those who designed the activity. But whatever the case, remember: *Decisions about games seldom are made in isolation; rather, one set of decisions always affects another set.*

Movement

Since all our games include movement, we strongly emphasize its many uses and forms. We look at the types of movements, where they are to be performed, how much or how many are appropriate, their quality, and so forth.

Naturally, the movements we select for a particular game are determined to some degree by our purpose(s). For example, if our purpose is fitness, we include movements that enhance cardiorespiratory functioning, strength, body composition, or other physical attributes (see "Types" in table 2.3). If,

Figure 2.3 Many movements may be appropriate for one purpose as in these fitness activities.

Table 2.3	Movement Component of the Games Design Model	

Types	Locations	Quality
Physical attributes	Personal space	Force
Locomotor or nonlocomotor	Levels	Flow
Reception or propulsion	Directions	Speed
Body awareness	Planes Pathways	
	General space	

Relationships	Quantity	Sequences
Objects	Number	Task order within an episode
Players	Unit of time	
Group	Distance or location	

for example, we are interested in developing body control, then we include body awareness movements.

In addition, it may be appropriate to decide where and how the movements will occur. Perhaps they are to occur in the participants' own areas (location—personal space) while maintaining a crouched position (location—low level) or in a larger area (location—general space) as the players move along different pathways, traveling in various directions. How quickly or slowly (quality) should the players move? Should the movements be performed with other players (relationships) such as with a partner or in a small group? Should the movements include manipulating balls, ropes, or hoops, such as dribbling a ball while running or jumping a rope while traveling backward?

What amount of movement will players perform (quantity)? Will each player have three shooting opportunities at the basket? Must each player jump rope for 15 seconds before returning to home plate? In a relay, will all players unicycle for 50 feet? Walk on stilts for 25 feet and then return to their own team? As with the other categories, the purpose of the activity among other conditions will influence many of your choices.

Objects

As we design a game, we usually ask what types of equipment or materials will promote the desired purpose. In many traditional games, the equipment itself directs the nature of the game. We also have opportunities to modify, replace, or perhaps eliminate existing equipment altogether if such changes allow us to accomplish our purposes while including all players. In table 2.4, we provide some possibilities for examining the types and uses of equipment as well as the amount and placement of it.

One means of organizing materials is to classify objects according to how they may be used. Children can move around, under, over, and through such things as mats, ropes, and hoops. For instance, they can do cartwheels on mats, around cones, or from one rope to another. They also can use certain objects, such as skates and unicycles, to help them move. You can combine

Table 2.4   Objects Component of the Games Design Model

Types and uses	Quantity	Location
Moving in relation to Hurdles Mats Ropes Balls Hoops	None One Several Many	Piece—piece Piece—player Piece—group
Being moved by Skates Bicycles Unicycles		
Sending away with Bats Hockey sticks Feet and hands Racquets		
Gathering in with Gloves Hands Lacrosse sticks Milk cartons		

the two categories "Moving in relation to" and "Being moved by," for example, by having children use ramps and cones to build an obstacle course and then navigate the course on skates, skateboards, and unicycles.

Some objects are useful for absorbing force and gathering in or deflecting other objects. Gloves, mitts, certain sticks, racquets, and scoops made from milk cartons are common examples. Similarly, players can use some objects to propel other objects, for example, sticks and racquets as well as bats for hitting, feet for kicking, and hands for pushing and striking. Indeed, with some imagination, almost any object can serve some purpose. Can you see possibilities for nylon stockings, repaired inner tubes, yarn, milk cartons and oatmeal boxes, deflated playground balls, old shoes, or broken baseball bats? We will suggest many ideas for using these and other pieces of equipment as we offer games in later chapters.

How do you determine how you'll use an object? Look at the game limits, skill ability of the players, desired outcome, and many other factors. For example, you can use a hula hoop as a target, base, or safe zone, or as something to throw, catch, or move through. You can use racquets to propel, deflect, or gather in objects. You can use a milk carton to receive objects and as the object to be received.

You should also think about how much equipment to use. You may decide to use none at all. Or you may decide to only use one piece. If you want to increase each child's time on-task and reduce waiting and setup time, consider the number and types of objects carefully. Remember, some children become frustrated and begin to act out when they are forced to wait for a piece of equipment or are expected to use equipment that is not geared to their developmental needs and abilities. (We'll look at these considerations more closely in the next chapter, because failure to make appropriate decisions in the area of equipment can result in disappointing game experiences.)

The final set of decisions involves where you'll locate equipment in relation to other pieces and to the players. Prior to its use, should the equipment be near or far from the players? How can you position and group equipment to make it easily accessible before and during play? If a player has limited mobility, can you place the equipment closer to that individual to provide greater opportunity for success? How could a lack of appropriate choices influence the behavior of the players?

Organization

Three sets of decisions require attention in this category: the pattern, number of players in the pattern, and location of each player (see table 2.5).

The first decisions concern organizational patterns, which are numerous and varied. Some games have a fairly well-defined structure with players in a line, circle, or diamond. Some have a more loosely defined structure such as randomly scattered, somewhere along one of the walls, or simply in

Table 2.5	Organization Component of the Games Design Model		
Pattern	**Quantity**	**Location**	
Defined structure File Circle Zone Diamond Undefined structure Random Near the fence	Even or odd Constant or variable	Players Group Objects	

personal space. A related second decision concerns the number of players in the selected configurations. Will each group have an even number of players? An odd number? Does it matter? Will the numbers remain consistent throughout the game, or can they change?

A third decision involves the location of players in relation to one another and of groups in relation to one another and to the equipment. For example, you may wish to consider the proximity of players as they await turns in a relay game. Some players may need to be far enough away from other players to short-circuit annoying behaviors. Or as they toss and catch a ball, it may be helpful to establish an appropriate distance between players. In some cases, these location decisions may be more important than in others. For example, we can alter major league baseball drastically by only slightly altering the distance from home plate to first base.

These are but a few examples of organizational decisions. They will become more obvious as you examine the games we present in later chapters. Note them carefully, because by preplanning organizational decisions and sharing them with your players, you can reduce the number, duration, and intensity of potential management problems.

Limits

All games have limits, or rules. The nature of the limits is related to what we expect of players and conditions imposed by the environment (table 2.6).

Some movements will be acceptable or necessary, others not. It may, for example, be acceptable to run with a ball in football, but never in basketball. It also may be acceptable to run to, but not through, the long jump pit. In some relays, it may be necessary to go around every obstacle, while in other relays it may not.

Table 2.6	Limits Component of the Games Design Model	
Players	**Environment**

Movements
   Acceptable or unacceptable
   Necessary or unnecessary
 	
Participation
   Acceptable or unacceptable
   Necessary or unnecessary
	Physical aspects
	   Geographic boundaries of playing surface
	   Equipment
	   Number of players
	
	Activity conditions
	   Time of play
	   Scoring
	   Rules

In some games, certain forms of participation may be acceptable or necessary, but not in others. For example, the form of touching that is acceptable, even necessary, in football is neither acceptable nor necessary in basketball. Similarly, in baseball almost an entire team is required to sit down for most of the game; in soccer this would be completely unacceptable. Thus, if a game is to be effective, you must communicate to each player the kinds of movement and participation behaviors that are appropriate or inappropriate for that game.

Let's look more closely, now, at how environmental conditions affect a game. These are the physical aspects of the situation as well as the game aspects. Physical aspects are observable phenomena such as boundaries, objects, and team size. Choices here certainly will affect movement time to waiting time ratios. To illustrate, with only four 15-player teams in a relay, the ratio may favor waiting. By allowing more teams with fewer players per team, the ratio shifts in favor of moving. A simple idea, yet not practiced often enough. It's no wonder some children get bored with some of our games! Why, for example, must there be 11 soccer players per team? Can you reduce the number? If not, why not?

It is necessary to make some decisions about limitations within the activity itself. How long is an inning? Three outs? Four outs? Five minutes? After everyone has a chance at bat? How long does the game last? Nine innings? Six innings? Until dusk? How can a player score? Ball in the hoop is two points? Twice in succession equals four points plus a bonus point? What is allowable—and not? Only two teams on the field? Three teams? Pass the ball only to players on the field? Pass to players on the sidelines?

We cannot stress enough that decisions you make in one category may require you to make additional decisions in the limits category and vice versa. Both games designers and players must understand this relationship,

Figure 2.4   Physical aspect choices will certainly affect movement time to waiting time ratios.

as games and how they are played do affect players' self-esteem. Indeed, the limits category can be especially useful as we discuss shifting decisions from the games leader as designer to the games player as designer. Later we will talk more about allowing players to create governing limits.

By now, we hope we have familiarized you with a means for analyzing any game through these categories that represent common aspects of all games. By focusing on relevant aspects of a game, you can begin the process of accommodating all players while also achieving the purposes for which you're using the game. The next step in designing games requires you to manipulate these aspects to actually change the game or create a new one.

Step Two: Modifying a Game's Basic Structure

In this step, you will begin manipulating a game's design. You will expand the components of the model presented in step one and add specific alternatives to change a game.

Analyze the Game

Your first task is to select any movement game with which you are familiar. Once you have chosen a game, describe it using the model in table 2.1. Do this by asking a series of questions such as the following:

- What is the purpose of the game?
- Who will play?
- How will players be grouped?

- How many in each group?
- What types of movements are necessary?

By continuing this process across all categories, you will separate your game into many elements.

Modify One Category

Your next task is to focus on a single category. For many of us, the movement category is the simplest place to begin. So imagine (create) some movement possibilities not already listed in the analysis of your game. As you list each alternative, avoid attaching a value judgment to it. Instead, let your responses flow freely. Why? Value judgments such as "No, that would never work," "That would break the rules," or even "What a great idea!" can impede creativity. Keep in mind that the intent here is not to discover the "best" alternatives, but simply to brainstorm. The following example may help you understand how to approach this task.

■ Movement Relay

Category to be changed: Movement

Alternatives

1. Skip backward.
2. Run backward, carrying a ball.
3. Ride a skateboard.
4. "Walk" on hands only.
5. Skip rope down alone; come back with a partner.

Now, repeat this exercise using each of the categories and components. It will take some time, but when you're finished, you will have generated many alternatives. After completing this task, you may feel comfortable proceeding to the next one. If not, repeat the task using another game that you enjoy.

Modify the Game to Meet a New Purpose

The next task is to select a game with which you are quite familiar and change the game's purpose slightly. Again using table 2.1, examine each game category and decide whether that category might help you accomplish the new purpose. Then in each of the selected categories, generate alternatives within any components that seem appropriate to you.

A word of caution is in order, however: We have found it worthwhile to proceed slowly, carefully, and patiently. It is also helpful to repeat this exercise with other games. If you practice this strategy rather than rushing ahead, you'll enhance your ability to create alternatives. Finally, don't be afraid to try out some of your ideas with willing participants.

Figure 2.5   As you brainstorm alternatives, avoid attaching value judgments to them.

I was in graduate school at UCLA during its basketball dynasty. I had reserved the gym to work with a women's physical education class, but several UCLA basketball players were using the court for a pickup game. I planned to ask them to leave. But, since some of the students in the class had been experimenting with games modification, they saw the male players as an opportunity to practice their newly acquired skills. Without hesitation, one of the women approached an especially tall, well-known player and challenged his group to a "game." The rules were simple: (1) the men's team would score points in the usual manner, while the women could score two points by making a basket or one point by hitting the rim or backboard; (2) the men had to score three baskets in a row for the points to count; otherwise, none of the three baskets counted; and (3) the men could not steal the ball from the women or block their passes or shots. The men reluctantly agreed, stating that the women were distorting the game. The women countered that they only were trying to level the playing field. The women then upped the ante: winners could stay and play, losers had to depart the gym. The men could not pass up such a challenge, and a lively, competitive game developed. However, held to the modifications proposed by the women, the men began to lose—badly. As they left, one was overheard complaining that the women had "warped the game." The women disagreed.

Let's look, now, at kickball. The purpose of the game as usually played is to provide exercise and fun for those who are good at playing it. We would like to change the purpose to providing fun and exercise for *all* the participants. To begin to accomplish this new purpose, we decide to decrease waiting time for the offensive team (those who kick the ball) so that more kids are actively participating for more of the game. We decide that the organization and limits categories might be useful in making our intended change.

■ Kickball

Category to be changed: Organization

Component: Quantity

Alternatives

1. Divide the kicking team into three subteams.
2. Divide the kicking team into four subteams.
3. Divide the kicking team into five subteams.

Category to be changed: Limits

Component: Players

Alternatives

1. Three subteams: one kicks, another performs specified fitness tasks, another rests. Continue at bat until all three subteams perform all three tasks.
2. Four subteams: one kicks, another performs balance beam tasks, another shoots baskets, the other rests. Again, continue at bat until each subteam has performed each set of tasks.
3. Now, can you create alternatives based on the last organizational change made?

By now it should be more apparent how changes in one category interact with changes in another. Summarizing to this point, we have

1. noted that certain sets of decisions common to all games require your attention,
2. clustered these sets into several categories, each with subcategories or components,
3. asked you to alter some of these components, first for the sake of alteration itself, and then to accomplish some stated purpose, and
4. reiterated that you should alter game designs if it will enhance all players' game experiences.

Up until now you have started to modify an already established game. With a bit of deliberation, knowledge that certain sets of decisions (e.g., players, organization, limits) will influence the nature of a game, and continued willingness to avoid imposing value judgments on the alternatives you generate, you should be able to create an entirely new game as well. Yet, at this point, you still may not feel comfortable about designing a new game. But don't be afraid to create something novel. Talent, genius, and instruction can help, but it's persistence that will really see you through.

Step Three: Managing a Game's Degree of Difficulty

Our introduction to the concept of degree of difficulty was from our esteemed mentor, Muska Mosston. Until then, like most of our colleagues and friends, we believed in a single standard of performance decided on by the teacher. Allowing other possibilities to exist bordered on heresy. Then Muska introduced to us his now-famous concept of the "slanted rope." As you probably know, he held a rope about two feet off the ground and asked children to jump over it. All were successful. But when he raised the rope slightly, several students could not clear the rope. He continued to raise the rope and at each subsequent height, several more students were excluded from the experience. Indeed, this approach always excludes students. However, when Muska slanted the rope (one end of the rope at floor level, the other end at waist level), everyone selected an appropriate height. Everyone was successful. Everyone was included! With inclusion came changes in performance, personal growth, and increased willingness to seek physical activity. The impact of this idea profoundly affected our thinking.

Although we could consider this third step a substep of step two, we choose to treat it separately because it deals directly with the continuums of skills, abilities, and needs that exist among games players. And by modifying a game's degree of difficulty (D of D), we can provide experiences that challenge and satisfy all players.

How to Change Degree of Difficulty

Once again, we find it easiest to modify a game by considering it from the viewpoint of the movement category first. You can increase or decrease the difficulty of a movement task by examining and then altering its complexity. To do so, you must first recognize that all motor skills are rather complex, that is, they have many parts. For instance, a tennis serve has the following components:

1. Stance
2. Grip
3. Ball toss

4. Backswing
5. Forward swing
6. Ball contact
7. Follow-through

Altering any one of these components can affect a person's performance.

Besides the movement itself, factors from the other categories of the Games Design Model can either limit or facilitate a person's performance. Examples include the size of the playing area (limits category), the size and type of racquet used (objects), the weight and diameter of the ball (objects), and the height of the net (objects).

Thus in managing D of D of any task, we can manipulate such things as the number of task components players must perform, the size of an object, the length of a lever, the amount of support available for performing a particular movement (such as riding on a unicycle), the speed of an object, the size and distance of a target, and so on.

A Three-Step Strategy

We have found it helpful to approach D of D through a sequence of three action steps:

• **Action 1:** Identify the factors that may limit a player's performance—if they can be managed by you or the player. Thus, even though a player's visual perception, for example, may be an important factor, unless you can influence it directly, do not list it as a potentially manageable factor. In the tennis serve example, some factors already mentioned were the player's stance and swing as well as external factors such as ball size and net height.

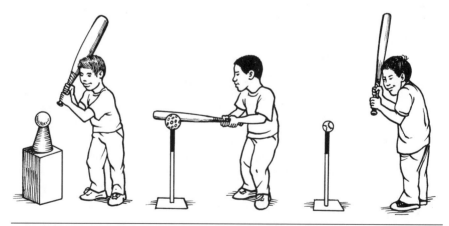

Figure 2.6 By modifying a game's degree of difficulty (D of D), we can provide experiences that challenge and satisfy all players.

• **Action 2:** You can make any task more or less challenging. Diagram a "task complexity (TC) spectrum." The spectrum is a continuum of task descriptors that you arrange from less to more difficult. For instance, a TC spectrum for the environmental factor "ball size" as it affects a player's ability to strike a moving ball might look like this:

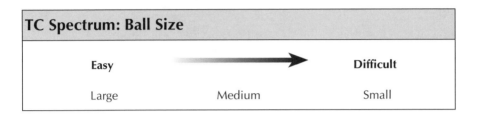

TC Spectrum: Ball Size

Easy		Difficult
Large	Medium	Small

From your own experience, you know that hitting a large ball is less difficult than hitting a smaller one. So even without an extensive background in analyzing movement tasks, with some practice, you can begin to diagram how you might make a task more or less challenging to a player. If you need further help getting started on this analysis, study the appendix, where you will find more examples of factors and TC spectra.

• **Action 3:** Begin to create tasks that vary in difficulty. To practice this task, let's continue to consider the TC spectrum regarding striking a ball. We have already thought about size of the ball as a factor to manipulate. Another factor is whether the ball is moving. Of course, a stationary ball is simpler to strike than a moving ball; a slow-moving ball simpler than a fast-moving ball; and a fast, direct-moving ball simpler than one with considerable spin. Thus, combining size with movement of the ball, we can create some simple to difficult tasks:

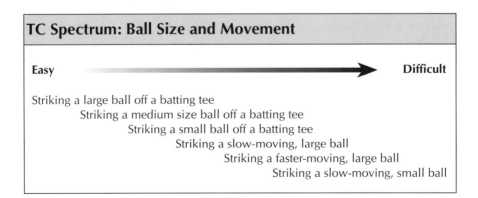

TC Spectrum: Ball Size and Movement

Easy ──────────────────────────▶ Difficult

Striking a large ball off a batting tee
    Striking a medium size ball off a batting tee
        Striking a small ball off a batting tee
            Striking a slow-moving, large ball
                Striking a faster-moving, large ball
                    Striking a slow-moving, small ball

Figure 2.7 Not all players need to play by the same rules.

Size is relative; based on your players' entry skill levels (the ability each displays when you plan to introduce the game), you must determine what constitutes large, medium, or small. Moreover, when you consider factors in combination (e.g., size of ball *and* whether it is moving), you must determine the relative importance of each factor. For instance, is it more difficult to strike a large, moving ball or a small, stationary one? If you wish to examine task difficulty and complexity in more depth, we recommend that you consult the appendix.

Using the TC procedure, you can create games in which players can engage in movement tasks compatible with their own movement abilities. In a softball game, for example, you might permit each batter to select from several bat lengths, weights, and grip sizes; from among balls of different sizes, textures, and colors; and from a variety of pitching possibilities, such as fast or slow, in a high arc or horizontal, and moving through the air or off a batting tee. As you can see, we generated each of these alternatives from the TC spectrum.

Along the same vein, ask questions such as, "Can a child with cerebral palsy who is able to move by using hand crutches join in a kickball game? Can you permit this player to strike either with a crutch, hand, or bat? Must she move around all the bases or can you allow her to move to another area? Is it possible to allow some players to choose among certain movements while giving other players different choices?"

We have offered only a few examples of the TC spectrum as applied to several areas of movement. Our intent is to show you how you can use the TC spectrum to modify varying aspects of games, accommodating a wide

Table 2.7	Modifying Degree of Difficulty Using Limits and Players	

Category	Modification
Limits	
Physical aspects	Can you increase or decrease the size of the playing area?
	Can you use different types of equipment?
	Can teams have different numbers of players?
Activity conditions	Can you have a turn-limit game?
	Can a basket be worth five points?
	Could you add up total points of both teams, and if they equal a predetermined score, declare a winner?
Players	
Characteristics	Could players of different ages and sizes play together safely and successfully?
Quantity	What happens if one team has more players than another?
	In soccer, could there be more than two teams on the field at the same time?

spectrum of player abilities. As mentioned, additional examples appear in the appendix.

Managing D of D Using All Categories

Movement is not the only means of managing a game's D of D, of course. You might also use another category, such as objects. To illustrate, in a basketball game, is it more difficult to dribble two balls at one time? Does the size of the object and its texture limit performance? Table 2.7 presents some additional games categories and points out how adjusting a few of the choices can impact a game's D of D.

As you can see, many, many possible alternatives exist in each games category. By managing them, you can design games that vary in complexity. The categories not only affect one another, they also interact and even overlap throughout. Therefore, you can juggle the three steps of managing D of D from the vantage point of any category, as long as you remember that factors from all the other categories feed into the one from which you're approaching the modification.

To summarize, the process of changing games involves three basic stages: understanding the basic structure of games in general, modifying that structure for a specific game, and then managing the game's degree of difficulty. Next, we'll share a specific strategy for using this process.

Table 2.8 Propulsion Skills—Kicking and Striking Profile

		Easy $\longrightarrow$ Difficult		
		C_1	C_2	C_3
Easy	S_1	Success 2/4/98	Success 2/5/98	Success 2/5/98
	S_2	Success 2/4/98	Success 2/5/98	Tried without success 2/8/98
Difficult	S_3	Tried without success 2/8/98		

Key: Object size (S)   Key: Object color (C)
S_1 = 12" rubber ball C_1 = Blue
S_2 = 8" rubber ball C_2 = Yellow
S_3 = 6" rubber ball C_3 = White

Player's name _____

A Strategy for Designing Games

Assuming you have some sense of what you want to accomplish with your players, you'll want to collect some pertinent information in relation to the players' current ability levels. Naturally, your purposes will dictate the type of information you collect. If, for example, you're interested in skill development, you may wish to observe players' movements and record their performances in some fashion. Many possibilities exist for gathering different types of information; some involve formal assessment instruments whereas others are much less formal. The idea is to collect useful information. As you know, many books and seminars are available on assessment, but here we'll look closely at an approach that works for us.

Table 2.9 Propulsion Skills—Factors Influencing Kicking and Striking

	Easy	⟶	Difficult
Ball size	Large	Medium	Small
Ball color and background color	Yellow/black	Blue/white	Yellow/white
Ball shape	Round	Oblong	Irregular
Ball movement	Stationary	Rolling slowly on ground	Rolling rapidly on ground
Angle of trajection	Horizontal	Vertical	Arc
Reception location	Body midline	Preferred side	Nonpreferred side

To keep records of player performance, you might consider creating a profile as demonstrated in table 2.8's example for kicking and striking performance as related to size and color of the object.

You can design profile sheets to include any performance factors you suspect to be important. But although you can examine multiple factors, we recommend beginning with only one. Then as you become more comfortable with their use, consider combinations. The tables in the appendix include degree of difficulty factors for 11 skills. You may use these tables to design profile sheets that include many different combinations of factors.

Once we know what the players can do, it is necessary to determine which variables likely influence performance. In the Games Design Model, the equipment and movement categories are often useful in this regard; we have already mentioned some of the variables that can influence, for example, a player's locomotor and reception skills. Table 2.9 identifies some factors that might influence the performance of propulsion skills such as kicking or striking.

This table suggests that it is easier to kick or strike a relatively large ball than to kick or strike a small one. Thus, as games leaders, we should offer players an opportunity to choose their own level of challenge by allowing them to select from a wide variety of, say, batting implements, objects to be batted, speed and angle of the trajectory, and so on.

Concluding Remarks

Depending on your goals, you may decide to use some of the suggestions we've presented in this chapter to make a game more or less challenging. Don't be afraid: Children in sandlots and backyards and on playgrounds have been modifying games haphazardly for years! By using the steps outlined in this chapter, however, you can design games that will enable you to achieve planned outcomes. The next chapter explores some strategies for presenting games effectively and inviting others to join your efforts.

Chapter 3

Helping Others Change Games

To change a game is one thing. Rousing others to do so is another. Questions that we hear most frequently include, "How do I instruct and encourage my players and colleagues to change games?" and "What tips can I give them about planning and presenting a game?"

A "Script" for Encouraging Others to Change Games

Most hesitations regarding altering and inventing games shouldn't surprise you:

- I wouldn't know where to begin.
- I've always played certain games in a particular way.
- I don't like that game, so I don't use it.
- I'm just not very creative!

Whether introducing the notion of changing games to colleagues or kids, you will face a similar challenge. How can you persuade them of the value of changing games and their own ability to do so? During the past 30 years of sharing our games design process, we have used a variety of strategies; often we've been successful, sometimes, we've failed miserably. But each attempt has been worth the risk. Indeed, it can be exhilarating to watch others realize their own creativity and find freedom in crafting games that accomplish particular purposes. When they understand that the limits of what is possible reside only in the mind of the games designer, a compelling energy enters the learning environment.

So how exactly do *we* share games design concepts with others? The following is a loose script representing one of many ways to encourage and instruct others in designing games. Of course, we modify the script according to the audience (e.g., kindergartners, teachers) and time (e.g., two hours, two months), but the general strategy has proven successful.

Concept 1: The Design of a Game Strongly Influences Each Participant's Experience of It

You can help your audience understand how games design affects game experience by playing the well-known game Simon Says. This game can, not only be fun, but also instructive. Before play begins, point out that the game Simon Says has two main purposes: to promote listening and following directions and to provide opportunities for practicing nonlocomotor and locomotor movements. Begin playing in the traditional fashion, but stop the game after a few people are eliminated. Ask the players why these individuals were removed from the game. Participants will usually respond that those who are now on the sidelines didn't listen or follow directions or were unable to perform the required movements. Then ask, "Now why are we playing this game?" Again, participants will say something like, "To practice listening and following directions and doing certain movements." When you say, "Who in this group do you think needs the most practice at doing these things?" the group will recognize that those who are no longer playing are also the ones who most needed to continue participating.

When we are following this strategy, someone usually remarks at this point that the game's design seems to defeat its stated purpose. That is, those most likely to be eliminated are the ones who might benefit most from continued participation. Then, we comment that one of our pet peeves is

Figure 3.1 In traditional games, it's often the people who need to play the most who are eliminated first.

playing a game and then formulating purposes, rather than the other way around.

We continue playing and quickly eliminate players with much gusto. Eventually we eliminate all remaining players by saying, "Simon says, 'Jump up'". . . followed immediately by " 'Come down!' Ah hah. Simon only said to jump up, not come down." Most players laugh or smile at the absurdity of the situation. Since no one takes the outcome seriously, a playful spirit prevails. But we have also accomplished a serious purpose: the players now understand that the game is designed for exclusion.

Next, we ask all players to rejoin the class (some require assurance that Simon Says is indeed finished), and we immediately play One Behind (see page 126, chapter 8). We review the previously stated purposes (e.g., listening, practicing nonlocomotor and locomotor movements) and attempt to reuse the movements used in the Simon Says game. A rule in One Behind is that if you forget which movement you should be performing, you may observe classmates and copy what they are doing. Designed for inclusion, the game is fun and accomplishes our stated objectives. Next, we ask players to comment on similarities and differences between the two games. Then, we underscore our main concept by asking, "Can you see how the design of a game can influence your experiences in that game?" Participants get the point!

Concept 2: There's More Than One Way to Play a Game, So Think of Alternatives

Why is this so important? Are we merely stating the obvious? Certainly, most of us recognize we can change any game. After all, we did so as kids. (Can you recall any "adjustments" you and other kids made to play a neighborhood game of baseball?) And then somewhere along the way we were informed of "*the* rules" or were told "Here is *the way* this game is played." We learned the right way, the only way—the single-standard design. Granted, in some circumstances a single-standard design may be appropriate, even necessary (e.g., professional sports). If, however, the purpose of your program is to include everyone, irrespective of ability level, experience, or motivation, is a single-standard design relevant? If you believe that your program should provide optimal challenges for every player, is a single-standard design beneficial? If not, might it be advantageous to explore the design of games more fully?

I was working with a group of teenagers, many of whom seldom dressed appropriately for physical activity and were considered by other instructors as "misfits." Instead of the prescribed activities, I introduced games analysis. We used leftover, abandoned, and broken equipment such as broken bats and partially deflated balls. We also used as much other equipment as possible (e.g., more than four bases, lots of balls of different sizes and shapes, large discarded orange cones from a local construction site). Gradually, as they embraced the idea of changing games, they invented a baseball-like game. To this day I don't understand all aspects of their game—but they did!

The game involved eight bases, a player could run in any order he or she chose; more than one person could be on a single base at the same time; three teams competed simultaneously; and batters selected not only the type of pitch but also the type of ball to be pitched. It was a crazy game, but it wasn't long before every player was thoroughly engaged in the process of games modification, wearing appropriate attire, and creating and completing related homework assignments. Through games analysis, ownership of the program had shifted to the players.

A suitable activity for emphasizing this concept is Couples Races (see page 120, chapter 8). We begin with a single design: in two parallel lines, partners face one another about 20 feet apart. The games leader asks all players in one of the lines to perform several movements. For example, "First shake hands with your partner, next run around your partner, then touch your right elbow to your partner's right elbow, and finally return to the start line. The race is over when each of you has returned and is waving to your partner." The role of the players in the stationary line is to encourage and assist their partners. After completing this race, we change the movements and partners' roles and replay the game. This gives players "permission" to play a single game in different ways as well as an opportunity to begin thinking in terms of alternatives. Then we repeat the activity until we are confident that players understand that a single game can include many variations.

When we ask about players' perceptions of the activity, a frequent response is that although a race, it is acceptable to finish last (no stated or implicit penalty). Another common remark is that the learning environment felt fairly safe because the only person watching was the partner, whose role was to encourage and offer support.

Our next step is to ask players for their alternative ideas. In general, asking groups to vary movements seems to be the easiest for them (versus limits, objects, and other categories). We select one or more of the suggestions and play the game again. We emphasize that the race isn't over until everyone is back and performing the last movement. This nuance can produce some interesting outcomes (players will tell you what they are). When asked, many players will declare that they are playing another game; some say, "same, yet different." As players become more involved in suggesting alternatives, we try out the suggestions, adjusting only for safety reasons. By encouraging multiple possibilities, we sanction that there can be more than one way to play a game. Though perhaps outwardly trivial, this is a critical step in becoming a confident games designer.

Concept 3: You Can Make Changes Within Various Categories

Using relays is a fun way to explore this concept. We design our first activity to focus players' awareness on the outcomes of traditional relays. We begin by running a "standard" relay. In column formation with six to eight players per column, we ask players to run down the floor, around a cone, back to their respective team, and then tag the next player. We repeat this process until everyone has had one turn. We declare the team finishing first the winner. Then we ask the group the following:

- What did you notice about this game?
- How many turns did each person get?
- Was anyone embarrassed?
- Those who came in fourth, fifth, last—how did you feel?

Players typically mention aspects of the relay they like (fun, belonging to a team, competition) and don't like (being last, being watched by others, having a single winner, getting only one turn, competition). Once again, they begin to reflect on their own experiences.

Now, we change the organizational pattern of this relay by shifting into a shuttle pattern. We ensure teams are only 30 feet apart from one another and then resume playing the relay. Often, we also introduce one change in the limits category (e.g., now the object of the relay is to see how many total individual turns each team can achieve within one minute). After the race, we ask the players what they noticed this time. Although responses vary widely among groups, we often receive comments about how they liked the changes, but were not as comfortable as in Couples Races where there was more support and less chance of being watched by lots of other players.

Next, we introduce the four-corners organizational pattern (see Four-Corner Relay, page 127, chapter 8). After teaching the players the traffic pattern, we begin the relay. At its conclusion, we note that simply by altering the organizational pattern (i.e., location of the teams) the nature of their participation shifted. We then give the first person in each group a playground ball and ask him or her either to carry or hand dribble it to the team diagonally across from his or her team, hand the ball to the next player on that team, and continue to the end of that team's line. Thus, we've introduced yet another change by altering the objects category. Depending on the group, we may continue with several more object changes. This approach makes the point rather quickly, however: altering components in games categories will change the game as well as participants' experiences of it.

Now that players have learned about the Games Design Model, making adjustments within games categories and seeing how these influence their experiences in a game, we guide them in transforming one game form (a relay race) into another game form. Using the four-corner organizational pattern and making changes in the categories of movement, objects, limits, and purpose, we introduce an entirely new game design (Lucky Seven; see page 134, chapter 8) with a correspondingly different outcome. For many players, this activity seems to confirm the strength and value of thinking in terms of alternatives (see also "Game Metamorphosis" section later in this chapter).

Concept 4: You Can Change Any Game to Accommodate All Players

The preceding activities may take place in a single session or across several days. We've learned that each group responds differently to new ideas; so we always have fun with the process, remaining playful. Since many games involve teams or large groups, we introduce the concept of inclusion within a team context. A guiding principle here is that any game can provide optimal challenges to every player sometime during the course of the game. To introduce this idea, our old standby is kickball. This game is often criticized by adults (even placed in the Physical Education Hall of Shame), but we demonstrate that a few modifications might render it suitable for most, if not all, players. We also mention at the start of the game that appropriate purposes (recall our pet peeve?) are to provide opportunities for running, kicking, catching, and throwing.

We begin with a traditional, "fourth-grade, no-nonsense, NCAA rules" game of kickball with the teacher serving as pitcher for both teams. "Regulation" rules include not allowing anyone to be put out by being hit by a thrown ball; in other words, only a force out, a tag out, or catching a fly ball are legitimate forms of putting someone out. Generally we play the game for about 5 to 10 minutes or until each team has had a complete turn at the plate (i.e., three outs each). We then ask the following questions:

- How many of you had a chance at the plate? (No more than six hands should be raised.)
- How many of you, on average, were ever involved in a single defensive play?

- Have any of you not touched the ball yet?
- Is it possible to change the game so more of you can run, kick, catch, and throw?

We encourage players to offer as many ideas as possible; and, for the moment, avoid placing value judgments on any of their suggestions, no matter how silly, unsafe, or absurd. Typically, we then try some of their ideas, yet sometimes we proceed directly to Maple Hill Ball (see page 121, chapter 8). This version of kickball was designed by elementary students many years ago. Since it is substantially different from traditional kickball, it may take several innings before players feel comfortable with it; yet, that is as it should be. To promote a fast-paced game, we have found it helpful to change from the traditional out-limited (i.e., three outs and then switch sides) to a time-limited game (e.g., after a team has been at the plate for two minutes, switch sides).

After 10 to 15 minutes of play, gather players and ask the same questions as before. It is important to merely listen again, avoiding value judgments about their responses. Most often some additional adjustments to the game will be necessary. Incorporate some of their suggested refinements (or perhaps play Maple Hill—Hit and Run; see page 123). Maple Hill—Hit and Run includes significantly more players in the offensive play. In fact, sometimes movement time is increased so much for everyone that we've had to build in recovery time! Once again, players notice that a modified game can produce markedly different outcomes and experiences.

Returning to the initial purposes of kickball, the variations thus far have allowed for more catching and throwing (each defensive player must catch the ball and throw to another player) and more running (now "platoons" of three or four kickers are at the plate at one time and, after the kick, they all run together). But only one player in each platoon kicks the ball. We now introduce the idea of degree of difficulty. After the ball is kicked and the platoon is running to the other end of the play area, rather than each of them jumping rope or performing a similar group task, they all have kicking opportunities.

We establish stations, each of which requires a different ability. For example, the first station requires kicking a ball through two milk cartons positioned 4 feet apart, 10 feet away. The second station is more challenging, requiring kicking a ball through two milk cartons positioned 3 feet apart, 15 feet away. At the most challenging station, a player must foot dribble a ball among several milk cartons without toppling any. Thus, each player can select whichever challenge is most appropriate for him or her. Naturally this requires a bit of cooperation, problem solving, and planning before the platoon arrives at the plate.

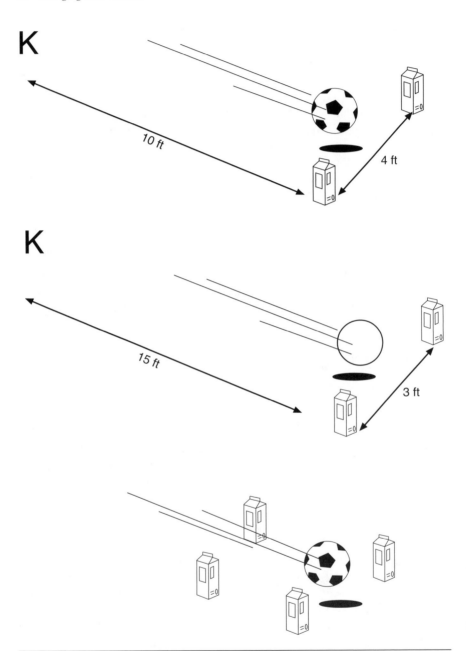

Figure 3.2 Providing alternatives gives players the chance to choose appropriate challenges.

Several years ago, I was teaching in a local elementary school. We were working on changing the design of games with our fifth graders. The class was comprised of a mix of skill abilities, interests, fitness levels, and cultural backgrounds. Ricardo was a quiet boy who always kept to himself. He was one of those kids who never bothered anyone, never interacted with others, a teacher's "dream"; yet, he also appeared lost and distant. The result is no one, not even his classmates, knew who Ricardo was! No one, including his teachers, expected much from him; what a missed opportunity for all of us!

Meanwhile, we began as a class to examine games and how they were put together and discovered that it was OK to change how we played games. The children formed groups, worked on solving design problems I proposed, and then offered their results in play. One day, all of the groups were stuck; they could not resolve a problem I had proposed. Absolute quiet and blank stares prevailed. They couldn't believe they were stuck, and then it happened! Almost inaudibly, Ricardo said timidly, "What would happen if. . . ." Everyone turned in astonishment. "Who said that? What a great idea! Why didn't we think of that? Wow!" Everyone smiled, acknowledging Ricardo with a torrent of appreciation. Ricardo dropped his eyes to the ground, and we all saw him smile, the first smile any of us had ever seen from him.

From that moment forward, the class learned so many things. Perhaps the most important being that a wealth of possibility exists within each of us, if only given the chance!

Most often, our next step is to identify a game, form a consensus on its purpose(s), and then begin to make changes across categories to accommodate the purpose(s). Imposing the notion of degree of difficulty on the entire process frequently leads to an exciting outcome. Players often carry the business of designing games beyond the schoolyard fence! They develop games notebooks and create their own homework (they call it "homefun"). At times, the two of us have little understanding about the intricacies of their games. Our roles become that of encouragers, skill developers, and sometimes arbitrators.

Game Metamorphosis

During just one activity period, it is possible to modify a game so that the original game is gradually transformed into a completely different one. For example, we have started with a game form called "relays" and through game design, shifted to another completely different activity form referred to as "creative movement." Let's take a moment and demonstrate one of the ways we've done this. Begin with the relay entitled Four-Corner Relay (see page 127, chapter 8).

Set the stage for the next major alternative by playing the relay game several times, changing the movement category of the game while emphasizing both locomotor and nonlocomotor movements. Next play some electronic music. Ask your players to listen to the music for only 15 seconds, suggesting to them that you bet they can move to the music in a variety of ways. Reset the group into the four-corner organizational pattern and assign each corner a number from one to four. Using the same traffic pattern as in the previously performed relay, direct each group to move to the group diagonally opposite their corner, one group at a time. As participants move across the playing area, have them interpret the music through their movements. When the last person in group 1 reaches the middle of the playing area, cue group 2 to begin traveling. Indicate to group 2 that they should each copy someone's movement from group 1. Repeat with groups 3 and 4. Then cue group 1 to move again when the last person in group 4 reaches the halfway mark. You have just shifted from relay to creative movement!

One thing you will soon notice is that no predetermined way a person is supposed to move to computer music exists. Consequently, any movement that is safe is acceptable. Another thing you will notice is that even those who are reticent about "jumping in" and performing are happy to play,

Figure 3.3 Blindfolding participants creates an easy, yet effective, variation in this game of Circle-the-Circle (see chapter 5).

because you permit them to copy someone else's movement. Thus, we have had great success with this activity. Children we present it to ask us to keep "playing" it after we've stopped the class. Now, experiment with this idea yourself. Can you imagine what you and your players might be able to create?

What Else Can I Do to Help Players Change Games?

As we and other games designers have experimented with changing games, we have used many of the following aids. As you read, think about how they might help you in your teaching situation.

Game Blocks

Using boxes similar to those available at most gift stores, select a category and write descriptors on each of the box's six sides. Reinforcing the edges with tape prolongs the life of the box (see figure 3.4). Use the Games Design Model (table 2.1, page 18) to help you develop descriptors. Make a dice set for each group, using the categories you wish to emphasize. To avoid creating dozens of boxes, consider constructing boxes with replaceable side panels. By sliding descriptors into the side holders you can constantly change information on the blocks.

As you can see, you can center descriptors around specific game components within each category. Players use the blocks as dice as they make decisions about the design of the game. Roll a die; the descriptor facing up becomes part of the game. This is a fun, nonthreatening way to introduce games design. After practicing with one die at a time, allow players to roll several dice at once. Certain combinations work well (e.g., movement types with movement quantity; objects types or objects quantity with location).

Figure 3.4   Game blocks.

Task Panels

Make a task panel from posterboard and cover it with a clear surface designed for use with erasable marker pens (see figure 3.5). You can change each of the descriptors within a category as the sessions progress from one day to the next.

In addition, you can copy this same information onto 8 1/2 by 11 task sheets and distribute it to individuals or small groups. Focus on designing the sheets to meet individual player characteristics and needs.

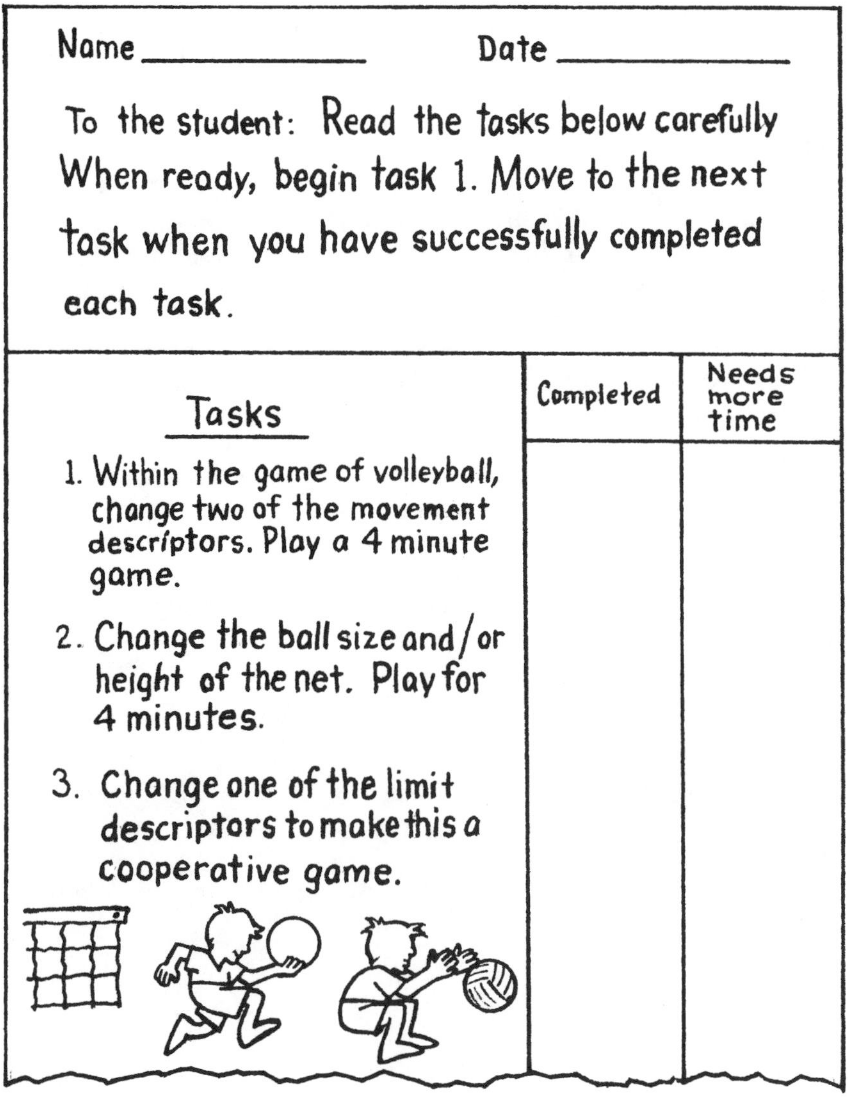

Name _____ Date _____

To the student: Read the tasks below carefully When ready, begin task 1. Move to the next task when you have successfully completed each task.

Tasks	Completed	Needs more time
1. Within the game of volleyball, change two of the movement descriptors. Play a 4 minute game.		
2. Change the ball size and/or height of the net. Play for 4 minutes.		
3. Change one of the limit descriptors to make this a cooperative game.		

Figure 3.5 Task panel.

Game Spinners

The basic concept of game spinners is similar to that of blocks (see figure 3.6). Using concentric rings made of posterboard, affix a moveable arrow in the center of all the rings. Each ring represents descriptors from one game category. Spin the arrow; the designated set of descriptors are those students will use in the new game (or those they'll change in the existing game).

While you can construct multiple concentric rings and simply interchange them as sessions progress, it is also possible to use material that permits you (or players) to constantly change descriptors. By rotating the position of each ring, for example, you offer new combinations of descriptors to the games designers.

Figure 3.6 Game spinners.

Game Surprise Box

The game surprise box works well with upper-elementary children (see figure 3.7). Allow each player to decorate a small cardboard box with stickers, sports and games heroes, rock groups, and so on. Place games design problems (or descriptors) on pieces of paper inside the box. In this manner, you exert some direction and planned change over the game, yet the players will control the game's final outcome.

Figure 3.7 Game surprise box.

Audiovisual Aids

You can use overhead transparencies to accomplish the same ends. For example, you can draw a game spinner onto a transparency. We have also had success using brief audiocassette recordings of game tasks with children as young as six years. How? Place cassette tape players at different locations in the movement area.

We hope all these ideas will prompt you and your players to generate many of your own. Don't be afraid to be creative!

Concluding Remarks

Remember as you play around with changing games that there are any number of ways to accomplish the same goal. We have shared with you some things that have worked for us these many years of working with children, and we hope that you will "try on" some of these ideas. But if they don't fit, kindly put them away. If they do fit, put them on and allow them to become yours. Begin the journey and enjoy it as you travel. Keep in mind along the road that our kids have learned that the real enjoyment is in the trip rather than the destination. Chapter 4 will offer more specific guidelines for making your travel plans.

Chapter 4

Understanding Games Teaching

Thus far, we've suggested that you can design and modify games to fit the needs of students and teachers, and we've presented some examples of games that have been successful for us over the past years. As we have shared these ideas with our colleagues, we have often been asked, "What approach should we use to present games to students?" This chapter will offer some responses to that question.

As you know, the most common approach used in the United States is to teach to a single-standard design game. If, for example, the instructor wishes to teach students basketball, she will teach basketball-specific skills, game rules, offensive and defensive strategies, and then, finally, will have students play basketball games—more often than not designed after a single standard. The lesson series presented prior to actual game-playing varies in length and substance, often depending upon the interests of teachers and students. Indeed, how many times have we heard, "Can't we just play the game?" Nonetheless, an instructor using the single-standard method attempts to sequence lessons properly by first addressing individual game skills needed in the target game, followed by lead-up games, and ultimately the game itself, often in a tournament during the last part of the unit. Sometimes an instructor will present the history of the game or sport as well. The focus of this approach is on skills and knowledge specific to the selected games and sports. This has been a useful strategy to employ in the upper elementary through high school grades.

Several observations over the years have led to the following questions regarding this approach, however:

- If you use a single-standard game design, will all students be included and successful?
- What are the skill levels that must be attained before you think the students should play the game?

- How much knowledge must a player possess about the game before the probability of success or enjoyment is high?
- Do you have time in a four-week unit to ensure that all students can attain the proper level of knowledge and skills?
- If less-skilled students don't reach the requisite skill level, can they and the more-skilled students successfully participate together in the game?
- What happens, then, to students' continued interest in game activity?
- Is the teaching focused upon the students or the game?

If your answers to these questions suggest that the traditional approach is not consistent with your beliefs, it is natural to ask, "Is there another way to teach games?"

Back in 1976 and again in the 1980s, we asserted that another approach is available. Colleagues in England—Len Almond, David Bunker, Lynne Spackman, Rod Thorpe, and others—have written a great deal about this subject. Specifically, the "understanding games" approach advocates teaching game appreciation and tactical awareness before teaching skill. This approach involves the belief that a player need not reach a particular level of skill before playing a game. Likewise, we can teach students to become aware of the decisions that must be made within a game while participating in it moment to moment.

Finally, this approach categorizes games differently. Rather than use skills, equipment, number of players, outcomes, seasonal sport, location, or themes as the organizing element, we suggest it is possible to develop games categories that have common tactical elements within them. Thus, we can meaningfully categorize games into invasion games, striking and fielding games, and net and racquet games. This approach enables students to focus on how to make the appropriate decisions within a game form as well as a specific game, rather than focusing on a particular technique specific to a game.

It gives us great pleasure to have an expert in this area, Dr. Kevin Taylor, share his work with us. Kevin has spent many years writing about and teaching games for understanding, and he has graciously accepted our invitation to share with you. Enjoy.

Rationale for the Approach

Games for Understanding (GFU) as an instructional strategy was originally devised in the late 1960s and 1970s by researchers and teacher educators at Loughborough University of Technology in England (Thorpe, Bunker, & Almond, 1984; Werner & Almond, 1990). Since its inception in the United

Kingdom, GFU has begun to flourish in the United States, where a number of educators have explored, tested, and explained the GFU model. During its development, however, researchers have used many different names to describe it. Perhaps the most common term used in the United States now is Teaching Games for Understanding (TGFU), but other terms include Teaching for Understanding (TFU), An Understanding Approach, A Tactical Approach, The Understanding Approach to Teaching Games, and Games-Centered Games.

Through observing and analyzing the effects of a traditional techniques-based approach to teaching games, the founders of GFU identified several important shortcomings of student performance in grade school physical education classes. Specifically, observations and discussions with teachers revealed that many children achieved little success in game situations due to instruction focused on individual techniques; the majority of high school graduates knew relatively little about game-playing; and those students regarded as skillful players, in fact, possessed inflexible techniques and poor decision-making skills and often depended on their teachers and coaches for tactical decision making (Bunker & Thorpe, 1982; Thorpe & Bunker, 1982).

In contrast, the GFU approach is designed to help students understand the game in the belief that they will then be motivated to play and learn the skills of the game. This approach makes intuitive sense when you consider that children love to play. And as proponents of GFU are quick to remind us, the first question students often ask when they arrive for a PE class is, "Are we going to play a game today?"

Perhaps even more important than the intrinsic motivation to play is the idea of introducing students to the context in which they are likely to use a skill. This makes perfect sense, because it gives them a reason to value that skill. Consider, for example, the push pass in soccer. Nowhere in a child's life does the ability to play a push pass have any relevance other than in a game of soccer. If a child has yet to understand or appreciate the need for fast, accurate short passing within the game, then why would that child want to develop fast, accurate passing? Therefore, creating a situation in which a child discovers for him- or herself the importance of making a fast, accurate pass is likely to be far more powerful than asking a child to accept this on faith. Thus, the aim of a GFU approach is to change a child's question from "Are we going to play a game today?" to "How do I do that?" When this change occurs, the child shows that he or she appreciates the need for improving technique and is motivated to learn the appropriate technique.

The Curriculum Model

In the traditional techniques-based approach to instruction, the instructor teaches students to develop technique and skills before progressing to strategies and tactics. In contrast, under a GFU model, the instructor introduces students to strategies and game concepts at the beginning of instruction so they understand the context for which they need to develop technical skill and ability. In its purest form, a GFU approach will not involve isolating and teaching discrete skills unless a student specifically asks how he or she might best perform a skill. Rather, the successful GFU teacher is one who can design a progression of lead-up games that gradually introduces students to the full game. So when you're designing a game's progression, you should address how you will help students develop an appreciation of the game, tactical awareness, appropriate decision-making skills, and knowledge of how to apply the skills in progressively more demanding game-like situations. Figure 4.1 outlines the progressive stages in the GFU curriculum model in contrast to the stages most often used in a traditional techniques-based approach.

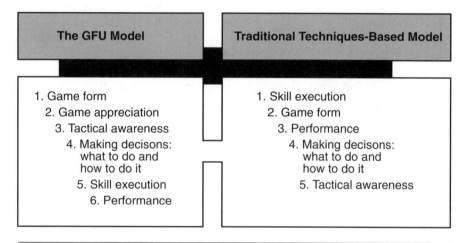

Figure 4.1 The Games for Understanding (GFU) Model compared with the traditional techniques-based model.

Stages of GFU Instruction

To fully understand how you might use a GFU approach in developing a unit of instruction, it is important to understand each element of this curriculum model:

1. **Game form.** The GFU approach begins with some form of a game. Yet, while the full game provides a long-term goal for both students and instructors, in the early stages of learning, it is necessary for the instructor to design forms of the full game that are appropriate for the age and experience of the students.

2. **Game appreciation.** Understanding the rules of any game is fundamental to playing; hence, learners should be familiar with the rules from the outset. Beyond rote memorization of the laws governing play, a GFU approach stresses the interplay of rules, skills, and strategies. For example, raising the net is likely to slow a game down and create longer rallies, reducing fielding players in a striking game will increase scoring, and increasing the size of the target used in an invasion game will make defense more difficult. A deeper understanding of rules and their interplay with skills and strategies is also likely to produce a more informed spectator.

3. **Tactical awareness.** The most marked difference between the GFU approach and a traditional techniques-based approach is the timing of attention to tactical considerations. In GFU, developing tactical awareness is central to the instructional process in that in any game this process hinges on finding answers to the question of how to win the game. Teaching to develop tactical awareness involves creating a progression from the most simple elements of strategy to the most complex levels of tactical game play. Where a traditional approach would address the fundamental techniques of the game, a GFU approach teaches the fundamental strategies. Thus, progression through a unit of instruction shifts from depending on the students' level of technical ability to their level of tactical awareness. In short, the GFU approach begins with the question "How are we going to win?" rather than ending with it.

4. **Making decisions.** One of the marks of a truly skilled games player is the ability to make quick decisions under pressure. By focusing on tactical awareness early in the teaching progression, you force students to think about "what to do" in the constantly changing circumstances of a game. Deciding what to do often involves choosing among more than one possible course of action, making it essential for the GFU instructor to provide students with multiple solutions to each tactical problem identified. Thus, as tactical proficiency clearly depends on the ability to make sound decisions, it is important that instruction delivered from a GFU perspective focuses heavily on the process of decision making.

5. **Skill execution.** The GFU approach does not ignore or in any way devalue the importance of developing fundamentally sound technique. Instead, the GFU instructor addresses skill execution through direct instruction after using and manipulating game forms to "set the scene for the development of tactical awareness and decision-making" (Werner & Almond, 1990). The intent of the GFU approach is that, once learners understand the tactics of the game and the usefulness of different techniques, they will ask for help in developing these techniques. Once tactical awareness and decision making have been addressed, instruction from a GFU perspective may seek to develop skill in much the same way as a traditional approach. Thus, developmentally appropriate learning experiences, designed to develop skill execution in tactical situations occurring within a

game, can be as much a part of a GFU approach as it may be in a well-designed traditional approach. What distinguishes teaching skills within GFU from a traditional approach, however, is that the point of departure into skill development is always from a tactical game situation.

6. **Performance.** The final stage of the model is essentially a reflective-evaluative phase in which the instructor examines student performance in terms of both skill and tactical proficiency. Here, the instructor should compare observed student outcomes to the criteria that determines successful and skilled performance in the full game. Specifically, in the performance stage of the GFU curriculum model, the instructor should examine both the appropriateness of a response as well as the efficiency of technique (Bunker & Thorpe, 1982). In short, at this stage, the instructor should be asking, "Has the learner reached the point of combining tactical proficiency with appropriate decision making and technically skilled performance?"

Games Development

As you well know, games form a major component of most physical education curricula. One of the assumptions of the GFU approach to instruction is that learning can be enhanced by capitalizing on the tactical similarities between and among different games. Drawing from a system of classifying games originally proposed by Ellis (1983), as mentioned earlier, the GFU approach divides games into one of four categories, based upon their tactical similarity: invasion games, net and wall games, fielding and run-scoring games, and target games.

Invasion games involve teams of players who intermingle in order to invade the opposition's territory to score points or goals. Within the category of invasion games, we can use subcategories to identify games in which the scoring object is controlled using hands, feet, or implements. We can also make one further subcategorization between focused target games, that is, games with a fixed goal, such as soccer, and games that have an open-ended target, that is, games with an end line that must be crossed, such as rugby or football.

Net and wall games, as the name suggests, include any game in which the playing area incorporates play over a net or against a wall. Unlike invasion games, net and wall games involve the strategy of attempting to place a shot or hit in such a way that the opponent is unable to return the object into play.

Fielding and run-scoring sports and games involve strategies that revolve around the concept of one team denying runs by fielding a ball and returning it quickly to a designated point or area.

Target games and activities constitute perhaps the only major weakness of the GFU model as strategies within this classification are far more limited and undeveloped (Werner & Almond, 1990).

Invasion	Net and Wall	Fielding and Run-Scoring	Target
Basketball (FT) Netball (FT) Team handball (FT) Ultimate frisbee (OET) Water polo (FT) Football (OET) Soccer (FT) Rugby (OET) Speedball (OET) Hockey (FT) Lacrosse (FT) Ice hockey (FT)	**Net** Badminton (I) Tennis (I) Table tennis (I) Paddle tennis (I) Platform tennis (I) Volleyball (H) **Wall** Squash (I) Handball (H) Paddleball (I) Racketball (I) Jai alai (I)	Baseball Softball Rounders Cricket Kickball	Golf Croquet Bowls Curling Ten (5 or 9) pin Pub skittles Billiards Snooker Pool
FT—Focused target OET—Open-ended target	I—Implement H—Hand		

Figure 4.2   Contrasting curriculum models.

Modifying Game Form to Highlight Tactical Similarities

In GFU, the instructor introduces games with tactical similarity in modified forms, focusing on specific tactical problems that exist within the game. Specifically, researchers have identified four fundamental principles of game form modification to use when changing games to highlight tactical similarity (Thorpe, Bunker, & Almond, 1984):

1. Sampling
2. Modification-representation
3. Modification-exaggeration
4. Tactical complexity

These are not necessarily discrete entities, however. But for the purposes of this discussion, we will examine each concept individually to illustrate how it is possible to use more than one form of modification simultaneously.

Sampling

The concept of sampling represents a fairly radical change from a traditional approach in that the instructor selects games based on their tactical similarity. Using the system of games classification discussed earlier, a well-balanced GFU curriculum would not be dominated by the more traditional team sports. A balanced presentation of invasion games would include games with a focused target, like basketball, team handball, and soccer, as well as games with an open-ended target, such as football, rugby, speedball, and ultimate Frisbee. The GFU approach teaches for transfer by sampling, or isolating, specific similar strategies and tactics from several games. For example, a learner who is struggling to recognize the opportunity to use "give-and-go" in basketball can practice the same move in soccer, ultimate Frisbee, field hockey, and speedball.

Modification-Representation

To be sensitive to varying developmental levels, as a GFU instructor, you must carefully structure modified game forms to ensure they contain the same fundamental tactical structures as the full game. In short, where possible, you should try to protect the essential characteristics of the game. For example, having fewer than six players in the field during a softball game would not allow the students to experience the tactical considerations associated with fielding. Instead, you may need to modify equipment and playing area dimensions to accommodate younger or lower-skilled learners. Thus, when you use miniature versions of a full-size game, you still will be introducing the same problems and challenges faced in the full game—but on a scale players can handle. As a final example, you could have students play tennis with paddles on a badminton court to work on tactical considerations associated with when and how to attack.

Modification-Exaggeration

In the GFU approach, distinguishing between primary and secondary rules is useful for modifying games. Primary rules of a game are those that provide the essential form of a game. In soccer, for example, the rule that prevents players (except the goalkeeper) from touching the ball with their hands is clearly a primary rule. Secondary rules, in contrast, are those that when manipulated may exaggerate the need for a particular strategy, thereby altering the nature of the game, but still preserving much of the essence of that game. For example, a game of badminton played on a court where one side is longer than the other leads the player in the short court to recognize that points can be won by forcing an opponent to move quickly from front to back. Note that a modified game may include both exaggeration and representation. As you can see, the skill of modifying games in ways that exaggerate appropriate tactical elements yet maintain a resemblance to the full game is crucial to success in the GFU approach.

Tactical Complexity

Tactical complexity varies a great deal among games: some games involve relatively simple tactical considerations while others are remarkably complex. Therefore, a GFU approach to teaching games should involve a gradual progression from simple to more complex games. For example, you might choose to begin with a "target-unopposed" game, before progressing to a net or wall game, followed by a fielding and run-scoring game (Thorpe, Bunker, & Almond, 1984).

A better organized games curriculum in physical education is an important element of the GFU movement, because the varying levels of tactical complexity within different games have far-reaching implications for the scope and sequence of games in the curriculum. From a GFU perspective, games education in a grade school setting becomes more than just playing a variety of different games loosely organized into a sequence that often matches the seasons associated with elite and professional sports. Instead, a well-organized GFU curriculum uses the level of tactical complexity within a game to determine a logical progression (Werner, Thorpe, & Bunker, 1996).

GFU Examples

To further explain and illustrate the differences between a traditional and a GFU approach, the following sections offer examples of activities you might use to teach badminton and soccer using a GFU approach.

Badminton

When you are about to teach badminton using a GFU approach, ask yourself, "What is my content?" Under a traditional approach, your content may be the grip, serve, overhead clear, and so forth, but what should your content be with a GFU approach? The major strategies and tactics of the game: playing into space away from an opponent, creating space for a winner by moving an opponent back and forth or side to side, maintaining the attack, and serving to weak spots in an opponent's defense.

When we reduce the tactical complexities of badminton to their simplest form, the initial content for a badminton unit bears a striking similarity to other net and wall games under the classification system described earlier. Specifically, games such as tennis, volleyball, and racquetball all involve striking a ball so that it is difficult, preferably impossible, for an opponent to return the ball into play. Indeed, experts in tennis, volleyball, racquetball, and badminton would all agree that focusing on playing shots that are difficult to return is an appropriate strategy for beginners to work on.

But there's a catch: If beginners are going to start by learning strategy, you must minimize the need for technically skilled movement so that a lack of skill does not prevent a student from using the strategy. For example, if a student has to concentrate hard on generating enough force to return the tennis ball in play, it is unlikely he or she will be able to devote much attention to developing strategy and tactics. But remember, in the same way that it is often important for a student to attempt a skill in order to fully understand the demands of that skill, a student is more likely to fully understand and appreciate the need for a strategy he or she has actually been able to use. In contrast, if you have a player start by using his or her hands to strike a high-density Nerf ball, you have reduced the prerequisite skills to the point at which he or she is able to think about strategies and tactics. Let's look, now, at exactly how to go about developing such a progression.

Hits in Space

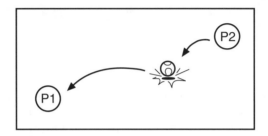

You can use this first game in the progression to begin teaching any net or wall game using a GFU approach, as it is stripped down to almost pure strategy! In Hits in Space, players use their hands to hit the ball either on the volley or from a single bounce as in tennis, table tennis, or racquetball. If the ball bounces a second time, the rally ends. The service alternates between players every five points, and players can serve however they wish and do not have to be serving to score a point. Players can make contact with the front or back of either hand, which they may cup or keep flat. If students have problems hitting the ball, you may even decide to let them catch and throw the ball. Remember, the objective is to let students explore the concept of trying to hit the ball in such a way that an opponent cannot return it.

Although students may need various levels of prompting by you, they will eventually discover that this game is extremely difficult to win against the serve. A wily server will serve the ball low and away from the opponent, leaving no chance of returning it before it bounces a second time. Thus, Hits in Space becomes somewhat meaningless once one of the players discovers and masters the strategy of serving and hitting away from his or her opponent. Then you can briefly demonstrate serves hit low and away from the receiving player to address the need for rules that create fair play. Adding a net will restore the challenge and allow students to focus on practicing other strategies common to net and wall games, which brings us to Squares.

Squares

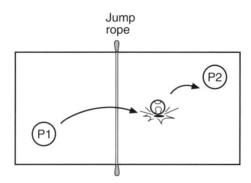

Jump
rope

Introduce players to the idea of a net gradually. After pointing out the need
for rules that allow participants to play and contest a game in a fair and even
fashion, add a jump rope to the marked area on the floor, dividing the
existing area into two squares. Note that this second game is still fairly
generic in that you could easily use it in a progression leading up to a unit
on any net or wall game. After students have mastered this arrangement,
add a low net, then move to successively higher and higher nets. Through
either a direct or an indirect teaching style, it is possible, now, to have
students focus on their positioning relative to court coverage as well as
positioning for attack versus defense.

Vary the court dimensions when students learn that by standing at the
"net" it is easy to dominate a game of Squares. This game is also valuable in
helping students recognize the need for strict rules governing the delivery
and receipt of serve to create a fair and even game.

As you gradually manipulate Squares to look more like badminton and
begin to address more specific badminton strategy, introducing badminton
racquets and a badminton court is clearly important. At this point, if
students truly understand and appreciate the strategies and tactics of the
game, then their desire to play the game may itself motivate them to learn
the skills necessary to apply the strategies they've learned to a more realistic
badminton setting.

Short and Wide, Long and Thin

A half-court singles game played on a long and thin court is a popular way
to begin building toward a full game of badminton. But while half-court
singles is an excellent game to use extensively regardless of the instructional
strategy you're employing, playing a short and wide court game is perhaps

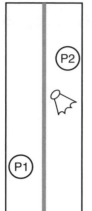

Short and wide

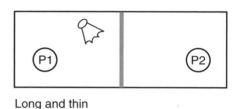

Long and thin

a better place to start. Using a short court and playing at the net acquaints students with a badminton racquet and helps them get used to using the wrist before moving to a long court where they need the wrist to help generate power.

Both long, thin courts and short, wide courts will encourage students to focus on using specific placement strategies to win the game. Of course, these activities are useful in a variety of net and wall games, particularly when teaching the importance of moving quickly to a base position after every shot.

Two-Thirds, One-Third

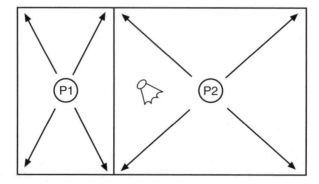

As court coverage improves and students are better able to return to the base position in between shots, an invaluable game for students to play is one in which the net divides the court into two-thirds and one-third. Two-Thirds, One-Third gives students the chance and time to explore how they can gain an advantage by moving the opponent around the whole court. At this point, though, it is essential to set up rules to govern how players earn the right to switch ends. Options include a set time period, a set number of points, or that every serve must be from the larger of the two ends. However you choose to regulate who plays at which end, remember why you are playing this game, namely to ensure that P2 works on court coverage and P1 works on using a variety of carefully placed shots that force the opponent to move.

In addition to moving the boundaries of the court to condition players to use specific strategies, you can also vary the height of the net you're using or you can set false markings on the floor that force players to hit into specific areas. Students may hit deeper clears, for example, if shuttles landing in squares taped into the rear corners of the court scored three points instead of one. To help students work on net play, suspend a string a short distance above and parallel to the net to force students to concentrate on playing attacking shots close to the net.

Concluding Notes

A common misconception that people form when they first encounter the GFU approach is that it does not allow for skill instruction. But as you can see in figure 4.1, which compares the GFU curriculum model with a traditional skill-based approach, the fifth element clearly advocates teaching skills. Although the sample progression we've provided does not refer to teaching component skills of badminton, it is merely an example of what is unique to the GFU approach, namely, beginning instruction with game appreciation and tactical awareness. Whenever players need to use a specific skill to apply a strategy, you should focus on developing that skill— once you have identified and taught that strategy.

Note, however, that the more indirect you decide to be in applying a GFU approach, the more you'll need to employ guided discovery techniques and the more willing you should be to wait for students to ask for help with the necessary skills. In contrast, if you choose a more direct way of applying the GFU approach, you will control when and which skills you address to a much greater extent. Even so, although GFU is clearly a more student-centered approach than a traditional skill-based approach, you may still need to curb the tendency to overdirect.

Soccer

Under a traditional techniques-based approach, the content of a soccer unit generally includes various forms of passing and receiving a ball, dribbling and ball control, shooting, heading, and tackling. Using a GFU approach, the content of a soccer unit may involve working on elements such as controlling the ball, supporting (depth and width), creating space, tackling, defending or denying space, defending the goal (shot-blocking, stopping), and concentrating on defensive roles (first defender, second defender, and so on). As with badminton, you should address the component skills of the game that are necessary to ensure, for example, maintaining possession, but only after paying careful attention to developing game appreciation and tactical awareness.

Maintaining possession of the ball is a central tactical problem in soccer. Without possession a team cannot build an attack and so cannot hope to score. Maintaining possession involves using both individual and team strategies. So in the same way that our badminton example began with activities designed to allow beginners to focus on basic strategies, the following progression of soccer games begins with a simple game of possession that allows students to be successful while working to develop group and individual strategies.

Keep Away

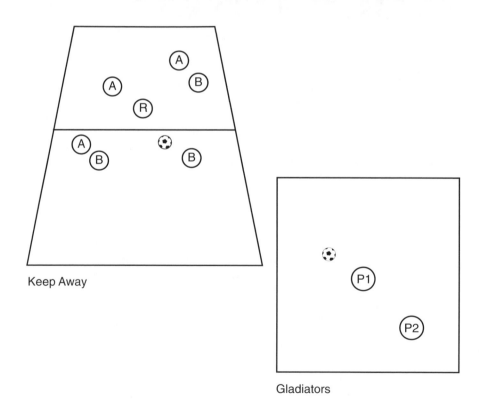

Keep Away

Gladiators

In a simple game of Keep Away, players can work on both small group and individual strategies for maintaining possession. To ensure some level of success while working with beginners it may be necessary to stack the odds in favor of the team with the ball by making the side uneven, say three versus two or four versus three. One way of keeping the game flowing but ensuring the team with the ball has more players is to create a floating, or rotating, player who always plays with the team in possession (player R).

It is common in Keep Away games for people to panic and lose their composure, often resulting in their losing the ball when a member of the opposite team challenges for possession. To help individuals develop a strategy for dealing with the one-on-one threat of losing the ball, a game of Gladiators, or one-on-one Keep Away, can be extremely useful.

Of course, similarities abound between soccer and other invasion games. So to teach for transfer, it makes sense whenever possible to use tactical similarities to your advantage as an instructor. Try, for example, having players pick the soccer ball up and pretend it's a basketball while playing Keep Away games. Certainly, if students have a better working knowledge of basketball, why not tie what you are teaching to something that they have already learned? Kids need to see for themselves that the concept of supporting a player in possession of the ball is essentially the same in a great variety of invasion games.

Give and Take

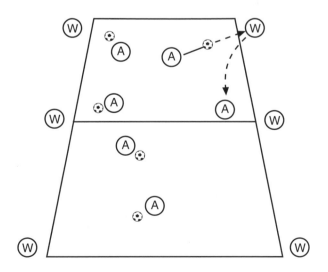

A game of Give and Take allows players to work on a variety of individual strategies for passing and opening up to receive a return pass, developing a player's ability to evade (get free) from an opponent who is marking (guarding) them. In a 10-by-20-yard area divided into two squares, supporting players (W) spread around the perimeter of the two squares providing attacking players (A) a target to pass to before evading an imaginary defender to receive the return pass. Attacking players (A) have a ball each and practice initially with imaginary defenders. Gradually add first one, then more real defenders to prepare players for situations in which, ultimately, they will all be individually marked.

Captains

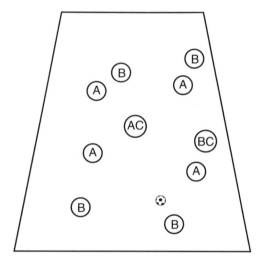

To continue working on the strategies associated with maintaining possession, play Captains, which challenges players to score by passing the ball to their captain. Divide the group into two equal teams and designate a captain on each team, distinguishing him or her in some way, perhaps with a different colored pinny or a hat. Rotate players through the captain role, because getting open to receive a pass often requires a lot of running. To make the game easier or more challenging, vary the dimensions of the playing area, the number of captains and players on each team, or the number of touches a player is allowed before having to pass.

Race Down the Line

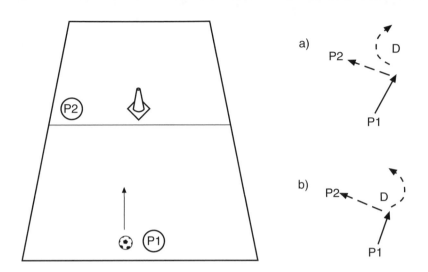

Thus far, we've covered maintaining possession as an individual and as a team, now we need to focus on maintaining possession while moving downfield. As with each strategy, introduce this one in as simple a form as possible. In Race Down the Line, players attempt to move from one end of a 10-by-20-yard area to the other as quickly as possible without losing possession of the ball. Initially, have players work with a cone representing an imaginary defender before progressing to including a defensive player who gradually has more freedom to move to attempt to intercept the attacking player. Progress further by encouraging players to explore different methods of beating the defender. As earlier, it may help students to compare this situation to basketball or another familiar invasion game. To beat the defender player P1 can (a) pass to P2, running between D and P2 to receive the return pass; (b) pass and run behind D; (c) fake the pass to P2 and dribble past D; or (d) take on the defender using fakes and feints.

Hit the Wall

This modified game combines everything players worked on in the sample progression thus far, allowing students to apply principles of support and

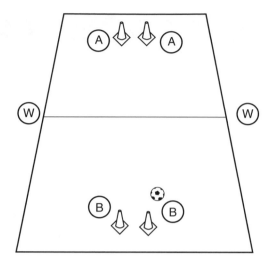

strategies for maintaining possession in a game structured for success. Hit the Wall involves players in a 2v2, 3v3, or 4v4 game with the corresponding numbers of players stationed around the sidelines to provide support. The object is to play a regular small-sided game of soccer with the exception that the team in possession may pass to supporting players (W) stationed along the sidelines. The figure above provides an example of a 2v2 game, hence there are two supporting players (W) positioned at the midpoint of the field, one on each sideline. Supporting players (W) act in support of whomever has the ball by offering an outlet. When a supporting player (W) receives the ball he either returns it to the same player or passes to another player of the same team. Specifically, Hit the Wall encourages players to use the full width of the playing area as well as apply the strategies they learned in Race Down the Line to a closer approximation of the full game. If a team makes good use of the supporting players (W), in essence they double the number of players on their team and increase their chance of success. Initially, supporting players (W) should be stationary and defenders should be forbidden from tackling them. As play improves you can modify this game by changing the number of players per side, allowing the supporting players to roam all or part of the sideline, and restricting the number of touches the player with the ball is allowed. Rotating teams from the field into the role of being the supporting players (W) provides each team with a "rest period" as they stand on the sidelines to offer support.

Further Modifications

At this point, your students probably still need to work on maintaining possession. So modify games to allow players more time in which to make decisions, thereby providing a valuable opportunity for developing decision-making skills. How? As you move children toward playing closer approximations of the full game, have them play small-sided games without tackling or dribbling. When players don't have to fear losing the ball, they have more time to control the ball and establish an appropriate passing target. Building on this concept, another useful condition to impose occasionally is a no-running rule. The prevention of running also gives players time to receive and distribute the ball without being pressured by a defender. There is also value in removing the right to run for a select number of talented players in a group of children with very diverse ability levels, allowing only the weaker players to run and forcing the stronger players to give the others more time while they walk. If you explain to the more talented players why they have been asked not to run, they usually take this as a compliment and feel special. However, if you suspect that singling out certain individuals is negatively impacting self-esteem, then you should immediately stop using this condition.

Review of Examples

In summary, if you decide to try a GFU approach to teaching any sport, you must first decide what you consider to be the most important, fundamental game concepts and strategies involved in the game. Then you must accept the challenge of designing games that will lead students to discover and master those concepts and strategies. Thus, rather than making your initial goal one of developing players who are technically proficient in performing component skills, your goal becomes one of developing players who understand the principles of the game and their role within their team's performance. But remember, a GFU approach does not exclude component skill instruction; rather, it simply advocates delaying this area until you have addressed the context in which players will use those skills.

So far, we have outlined some important aspects of the GFU approach: the need to design fundamentally sound drills and practices that are developmentally appropriate and to organize these drills and practice into a progression from simple to complex. But let's not forget that it is essential that GFU games themselves also be developmentally appropriate. For example, while it might be inappropriate to work on the principle of creating space in soccer with a group of third graders, it is reasonable to focus on having them spread out.

Putting GFU in Perspective

If you think about how physical educators often teach games using a traditional method, it should be easy for you to imagine how GFU got started. As you know, a fairly typical approach to teaching games within a traditional techniques-based orientation involves a lesson that has an introduction, an isolated skill or technique phase, followed by a game form which, more often than not, is far too advanced for the majority of learners in the class (Turner 1996). Unfortunately, a traditional approach breaks severely from a developmentally appropriate progression as instruction moves quickly from isolated skill practice to a fairly close approximation of the full game.

If learners are ultimately going to be successful in applying their talents within a game, it is essential that you allow them to practice applying their techniques in gradually more complex game forms. Certainly, educators have long been aware of the need to "teach for transfer." If learners are attempting to master a skill or technique they will ultimately employ in an environment other than the one in which they are learning it, you need to structure your instruction to facilitate transfer from the practice environment to the performance environment.

Upon close analysis, the shortcomings of a traditional techniques-based approach seem to hinge largely upon the apparent failure of instructors to design experiences that provide a gradual progression from isolated skill practice to successful application within a game. As indicated earlier, the inability to apply techniques within a game may be due to either a lack of proficiency in performing the technique under game conditions or to a lack of appreciation for the tactical considerations within that game. Students might also learn to appreciate tactics, understand game principles, and apply technique through a more traditional approach to instruction if the instructor integrates tactical considerations along with skill.

Researchers developed the GFU approach because traditional games instruction was ineffective, but what if the fault lies not with the traditional approach itself but with the way it is typically used? Indeed, a well-designed and appropriately implemented traditional approach includes the same elements that occur within a GFU approach, including teaching for transfer and paying close attention to developing tactical appreciation early. What is important to recognize here is that a poorly implemented or incomplete GFU approach that does not involve a gradual progression from simple to complex could be as weak and ineffective as a poorly implemented traditional approach. So if you are planning to adopt a GFU approach, be sure to thoroughly plan your progression, including paying careful attention to all the elements of the curriculum model outlined earlier.

A Continuum of Instructional Styles

If you are attempting to change your teaching style, it is important to recognize that the contrasting styles represented by a GFU and a traditional approach do not exist as isolated entities. Instead, a continuum exists between a traditional approach to games instruction, which begins by

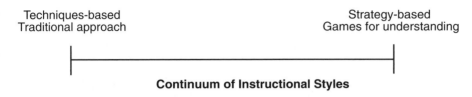

Continuum of Instructional Styles

Figure 4.3   The GFU approach and the traditional approach do not exist as isolated entities.

focusing on discrete and isolated skills, and a more "constructivist" approach, which begins by teaching game concepts and strategies. In all likelihood, if you're trying a GFU approach for the first time, you will adopt an approach to instruction that falls somewhere between the traditional and true GFU approach. Certainly, moving gradually from what is familiar into a new and different approach to instruction is perhaps the most sensible action, given the harsh realities of teaching in today's schools. It may even be wise to use GFU with one group and a more traditional approach with another group or perhaps teach different units from contrasting perspectives.

A growing body of literature thoroughly addresses how to implement a GFU approach to teaching. So if you are seriously considering changing your instructional style, be sure to explore the references. Start with *Teaching Sport Concepts and Skills: A Tactical Games Approach* by Griffin, Mitchell, and Oslin (1997). Particularly in the last chapter of their book, they offer a great deal of sound advice for anyone who is just getting started teaching from a GFU perspective.

Concluding Remarks

Make no mistake, you should not take the process of adopting a new and different approach to instruction lightly. An incomplete and poorly conceived curriculum will not be successful whether it is based on a traditional or GFU approach to instruction. Proponents of GFU frequently cite the shortcomings of a traditional approach as the main reason for change, but their criticism always paints a picture of an ill-conceived and incomplete traditional approach. A well-designed and appropriately implemented traditional curriculum would not be guilty of the shortcomings often used to justify GFU, however, so don't consider GFU a panacea for the ills that currently plague physical education.

Still, developing alternative approaches to instruction is a natural reaction to the changing faces of society and the educational system that exists within that society. Indeed, the fundamental tenets of GFU do not appear to be very far removed from those that are central to the growing support for a more constructivist approach to education; hence, we could say GFU takes a constructivist approach to teaching games. When grappling with these issues, remember, change is inevitable; positive change is an option open to those prepared to work hard at embracing and capitalizing upon change. And GFU represents an exciting possibility for physical educators who are committed to bringing about such positive change.

Part II Examples of Game Changes

Anyone can change a game, even create one. By this point in the book we hope you are convinced that games are not sacrosanct. In fact, an avid games designer sees dozens of possibilities for new games in any existing game. Indeed, during the past two decades, we have witnessed hundreds of children and adults devise literally thousands of games.

In this section, we will present some familiar game forms as well as a few novel ones. All these games have been designed by children and adults in various countries and cultures and played by real kids, who have enjoyed them in either their present format or with appropriate modifications.

To meet the needs, abilities, and interests of your players, you may need to make some adjustments in these activities; sometimes these adjustments will be minimal, other times dramatic. If you do choose to make changes, you may wish to review some of the procedures that we outlined in part I.

To help you review how to use the games categories to make changes, we have preceded each sample variation with a code indicating the categories (or category) of change used in that variation. The table below lists the abbreviation for each category.

Sample Variation Categories

PU	Purposes	**O**	Objects
PL	Players	**OR**	Organization
M	Movements	**L**	Limits

We present each game in a consistent format; that is, we name the game, suggest necessary resources such as equipment and materials, describe the game, and offer a few sample variations. Then, by using the strategies suggested in part I to alter the degree of difficulty and to include all players, you should be able to create many more variations for each game that we present. With your continued input, your personal "game bank" can increase dramatically.

Chapter 5

Adventure Games

$\int$ince the late 1970s, Project Adventure has been the leader in developing a multitude of adventure games used in programs across the nation. Typically, adventure games are educational activities that promote community, communication, trust, cooperation, team building, group problem solving, and leadership skills, all "within a matrix of high level enjoyment—often called fun" (Kissler, 1994, p. iv). The objectives and goals of these games vary according to the people who are involved, however; it all depends on which games an instructor uses and how he or she organizes and presents them.

Whether you call them *outdoor education*, *adventure education*, *play education*, or *challenge education*, the adventure games presented in this chapter are frequently used for facilitating group dynamics and a sense of community, steering players toward introspection, and challenging them in team tasks that involve decision making, consensus, and leadership. As with any game, however, when an adventure game's design changes, the game might serve a different purpose. So alter them carefully to ensure they meet your program's stated goals and objectives.

Circle-the-Circle

Equipment

2 large hoops per group

Description

1. Divide students into groups.
2. Have each group of students stand in a circle holding hands.
3. Hang two large hoops together between two people, resting hoops on their grasped hands.
4. Explain that the object of this game is to pass the hoops quickly around the circle in opposite directions. Players must pass over each other (and at some point through the other hoop) until they return both hoops to the starting point.

Sample Variations

L – In the order listed, assign each player in the circle one of the following disabilities: first person may not use legs (must sit down), next person cannot see (blindfolded), and third is mute (cannot talk); that is, "You can't see, you can't talk, sit down, you can't talk, you can't see," and so on.

O – In addition to the changes made in the first variation, replace the hoops with either a three-foot piece of bungee cord tied into a circle or a bicycle inner tube (with valve cut out) with ends tied in a knot.

O – Add another hoop.

OR – Instead of a circle, have players form columns. Each must join hands by bending over and reaching between his or her legs to grasp the outstretched hand of the person behind. Each column then passes a hoop from front to back.

L, M – Use the same organizational pattern as in the previous variation, but now besides passing the hoop from front to back, direct the entire column to also move from one location to another. When the hoop gets to the last person in the column, that person runs to the front of the column, which permits the column to advance forward.

OR – Have players stand with their backs toward the center of the circle.

L, OR – Have teams compete with the other circles to see how fast they can get the hoops around their circle.

Animal Game

Equipment

Description

1. Have players stand in a circle, close enough to reach their neighbors without straining.

2. Designate a player as IT and have this person stand inside the circle.

3. Direct IT to quickly point to a player standing in the circle and say either "elephant," "moose," or "rabbit" (see page 80).

4. Meanwhile, players must form the animal before IT can count to 10.

5. If the action is not completed by any one of the three players or if any one of the three forgets or makes the wrong move (IT decides what's correct, and no one is allowed to refute IT's decision), then have IT take that player's place in the circle, and designate the player who made the error as the new IT.

Animal Game Ideas

Moose: The player at whom IT points must quickly form a snout by extending both arms forward, hands clasped. At the same time, the two players to the immediate left and right of the snout must stretch out their arms to form antlers.

Elephant: Middle person forms trunk by reaching forward with one hand and, with the other hand, reaching underneath the outstretched hand and grasping one's own nose. Of course, once in that position, the player must swing the trunk about. Adjacent two players must simultaneously cup their hands next to the trunk person and flap these ears.

Rabbit: Middle person hops up and down, while person to left and person to right stomp the left and right foot, respectively.

Sample Variations

PL – Use only two animals, for example, elephant and giraffe.

M – Simplify the gestures, for example, elephant is formed by middle person placing fists in front of face, and players on each side cupping nearest hand behind middle person's ears.

L – Add or substitute animals, for example, cow: middle person interlaces fingers and points them downward, while children on either side grab a thumb and mime the milking motion, all *mooing*, of course. Let children design their own animals.

L – Have IT say the person's name before declaring an animal.

L, PL – Put two ITs in the center at the same time.

L – Substitute other roles for animals, for example, name three patriots: fife player, flag carrier, and drummer.

Keypunch

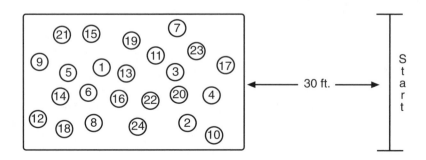

Equipment

90-foot rope, gym spot markers (or tennis can tops) numbered sequentially (1 to 24)

Description

1. Use the rope to create a rectangular "keyboard" inside of which you place the numbered spots. Orient spots randomly up and down the rectangle in a zigzag fashion, with all the odd numbers on one side and all the even numbers on the other side. It should not be obvious to the children that you have separated the odd from the even numbers (see diagram).

2. Designate a planning area 30 feet away, from which the group must "debug the computer" by physically touching all 24 numbered spots in sequence. Allow the group three attempts, timing each attempt and limiting total time to 20 minutes (or three attempts, whichever comes first). Begin timing when the first player leaves the playing area and end when the last returns. Only one player may be on the keyboard at a time, and he or she must touch numbers *only* in sequence. Violation of either rule results in a 10-second penalty.

Sample Variations

L – Place numbers inside the keyboard completely at random.

L – Allow only one player (or two or three) to touch spots in any given group attempt. The remaining players must discover a way to help these players.

O, L – Do not allow anyone to enter the keyboard. Rather, players must touch all keys with objects (e.g., balls or beanbags) they toss. Misses result in added time penalty.

M – Same as the previous variation, but designate the propulsion method to use.

L, OR – Vary the distance from the start area to the keyboard.

L, O – Substitute letters for numbers. Direct students to touch letters in alphabetical order or to spell a word or phrase.

OR – Have partners connected with one another move about the keyboard.

Traffic Jam

Equipment

carpet squares, gym spot markers or any other floor or ground markers (one more than the total number of players)

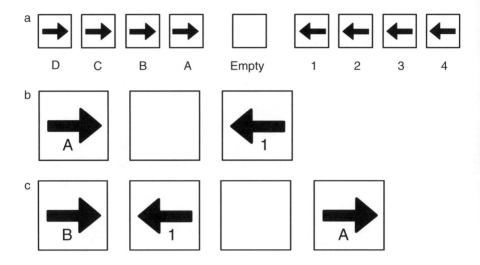

Description

Place the markers an easy step from one another in two lines with the extra square in the middle between the lines (see diagram).

1. Divide the group into two equal teams and have both face the middle unoccupied square (a).

2. Explain that the object is to have the two teams exchange places on the line of markers, using the extra marker. Using the following moves, players on the left side must end up in the places on the right side, and vice versa. Only one player may move at a time. That player has two options: (1) to step onto an empty marker that is directly in front of him or her or (2) to step onto an empty marker that is behind a player that is facing him or her. Thus, (b) either player A or player 1 may move onto the empty marker (because it is directly in front of each of them) and (c) player B may now move to the empty marker, because player 1 is now facing him or her.

3. Explain that it is illegal, however, for any player to move backward, around someone who is facing the same way he or she is (if you are looking at his or her back), or to move when someone else is moving.

Sample Variations

L – After the teams solve the problem once, play again, asking one individual to give all commands (all other players remain silent).

L – Once the problem is solved, have players return to their original positions, following the same rules, but without talking.

OR – Place markers (carpet squares) in a "V" or "U" shape; this helps students conceptualize the problem.

L – Have two separate groups perform the same task concurrently and, toward completion of the task, share whatever they learn with the other group.

OR – Try a circle.

OR – Have groups compete to see who can exchange places fastest.

Blind Polygon

Equipment

90-foot rope, blindfolds

Description

1. Have players stand in a circle, each blindfolded and holding the rope against his or her lower back with both hands.
2. Direct the group to form a square, explaining that players may not remove their hands from the rope or their blindfolds until the group decides that they have correctly formed a square.

Sample Variations

L – Have the group form a different polygon, such as a triangle or rectangle.

L, M – Same as first variation, but once the polygon is complete, direct the group to move it intact to a different location, still wearing their blindfolds.

L, M – Have each student first put on blindfold, and then, as a group, locate a piled-up rope before proceeding to form a polygon.

L, O – Same as previous variation, but do not allow group member to touch while they locate scattered objects, which they then organize into a polygon. Do not allow students to place objects closer than three feet from adjacent objects.

O – Without a rope, form the polygon by joining hands.

L – Have students make sounds, such as a beeping noise, to help them locate objects or each other.

OR – Alternate front-back positions of students in the group, for example, player 1 is facing forward, player 2 has back toward the center of the group.

L – Set a time limit.

TP Shuffle

Equipment

30-foot telephone pole (TP) placed horizontally on a level area, blocked so it can't roll (or attach each end to a vertical post or stump)

Description

1. Divide into two groups of 8 to 10.
2. Have each group balance on opposite ends of the pole.
3. Direct the two groups to exchange places on the pole without touching the ground.

Sample Variations

L, PU – Time the event and attach penalties (e.g., 10 seconds) each time a player touches the ground. Encourage the group to discuss the merits and shortcomings of their attempts, and then try again to beat their own personal bests.

L, OR – Have a single group line up along the pole and then rearrange themselves according to birthdate (or height, gender, grade level, shoe size, or the like) without touching the ground.

L – Same as previous variation, but direct group to perform the task nonverbally.

O, L – Same as previous variation, but use a four-by-four-inch beam or post and ask players to close their eyes (or wear blindfolds) throughout the problem. For protection, have each player assume the "bumpers up" position (hand in front of face, palms outward).

L, O, OR – Arrange eight-foot sections of four-by-four-inch beams in a square, hexagon, or the like. Do not allow players to pass one another at beam junctions.

O – Use a long jump rope, laid on the ground, or two parallel long jump ropes, six inches apart from one another.

L, PU – Have the students write in their journals about the nature of cooperation after playing any version of this game.

Chapter 6

Academic Games

These games are designed to supplement (not replace!) activities in academic areas such as science, math, writing, and reading. Each game entails specific academic operations and concepts. Why should you include these games? Because they include everyone regardless of ability, help students practice academic skills, and incorporate movement. Besides—they're fun!

This type of activity is not new, however. Educators such as Bryant Cratty and James Humphrey popularized academic exercises coupled with movement activities in the 1960s and 1970s. Indeed, we continue to see Cratty's *Active Learning* (1976) used in classrooms today.

The games contained in this chapter, however, differ from those just mentioned in one critical regard: Each is presented in the framework of modifying activities. You will be able to develop many variations from the few examples we provide, so you can create many academic games for a variety of subject areas. Our intent here is to provide you with some samples that represent *how* to modify academic games. Work with the classroom teachers in your school to choose appropriate material and individualize it efficiently.

Animalia

Equipment

50 cards per team—on each front, write 1 of the characteristics of 1 of 4 types of animal (see pages 89-90) or the name of the animal, and on the back, write the classification (for self-checking purposes); 1 animal classification board per team (columns labeled amphibian, mammal, reptile, bird, and then 4 blank spaces under each column)

Description

1. Give each team a classification board.
2. Place cards face up in a stack.
3. Direct one player from each team to run to the card pile, take the top card, and then place the card under the matching animal classification on the board. Explain that to check the answer, turn the card over. If the child places the card in the incorrect section on the board, he or she must return it to the bottom of the stack.
4. The next player repeats this process; if the player doesn't find a vacant space for the card, he or she must return it to the stack.

Sample Variations

O, L – Substitute other classifications (e.g., instead of animal types, substitute traditional Native American homes such as pueblo adobe, Arctic igloo, Northwest plank house, Central Plains tepee) and respective characteristics (e.g., living habits: nomad, settled; rain: large amounts, little, none; climate: warm, hot, cold; trees: large, small, none; food acquisition: mainly farmers, hunters, fishermen, or gatherers). Another substitution might be types of trees, and then identifying characteristics such as leaves, bark, buds, flowers, and fruit.

O, L – Create a board similar to that in the first variation, except now provide duplicate cards with each characteristic (e.g., two cards with a maple leaf, two with an oak leaf, two with a ginkgo leaf), and then, with cards facing down, have each student turn over two at a time. If they match and the student can identify the type of leaf correctly, the player or team keeps both cards. If the cards do not match or if the leaf has been incorrectly identified, the student must replace the cards face down. Whoever has the most cards when all the cards have been taken wins.

O, L – Omit cards. On board, list categories along the top as before, but now also list categories along the side as well. Explain that the purpose is for a team to correctly fill in as many blank spaces as possible in a specified time. For example, if one heading on a column is amphibian and one row heading is eggs, then a correct answer for the blank box for that column and row might be "laid in water" or "usually jelly-like."

O, L – Alter the difficulty of this last variation by changing the number and challenge of headings for columns and rows. For instance, one group might get columns entitled lizard, seagull, and bear, while another group gets these and also chipmunk and bat. In addition, the first group gets row headings concerning habitat components such as food and shelter, whereas the other group's board also includes prey. Or, instruct different teams to omit certain columns or rows from their boards.

M, PU – Dictate the locomotor movements to and from the cards.

OR – Have students work as partners.

OR – Have one class challenge another class to see who is the fastest.

Information for Animalia Cards

Mammal

Female provides milk for her young

Constant body temperature

Has at least some hair or fur

More complex brain

Blue whale

Porpoise

Otter

Mole

Bat

Mink

Bird

Has feathers

Streamlined body

Most can swim, climb, walk, and perch

May migrate in spring and fall

Pheasant

Robin

Kingfisher

Goldfinch

Reptile	Amphibian
Cold-blooded	Eggs usually jelly-like
Skin with horny scales	Eggs laid in water
Eggs have a hard or leathery skin	No visible scales
Lays eggs	Skin usually moist
Alligator	Lives in the water most of the time
Crocodile	Frog
Snake	Toad
Lizard	Salamander
Turtle	Newt

Shared Characteristics

Constant body temperature (mammal, bird)
Cold-blooded (reptile, amphibian)
Lays eggs (bird, reptile, amphibian)
No visible scales (bird, amphibian, mammal)

All-Fours Circle Math

Equipment

Description

1. Direct teams of 5 to 10 players to lie on the floor in a circle, with heads toward the center.

2. Begin the game by assigning each team member a number.

3. Announce a math problem (e.g., 2 + 2 = ____). In each group, the player whose assigned number corresponds to the correct answer gets up, jumps over everyone in the group, and returns to the start position.

Sample Variations

L – Give each player two numbers.

OR – Vary the start positions of the players (e.g., on hands and knees; lying face up with feet in the center of the circle).

M – Have moving players weave around the players rather than jumping over them.

L – Vary the math operation, for example, fractions, decimals.

OR – Have partners work together.

OR – Direct players to move around more than one circle.

The Number Grid

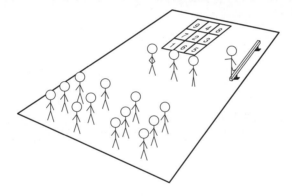

Equipment

beanbags, balance beam, large number grid (can be made out of plastic painter's drop cloths or black lawn plastic and solid-colored Con-Tact paper or colored tape)

Description

1. Line up teams of four to six players some distance away from the grid (see diagram).

2. Have each team send one player at a time to the grid.

3. After throwing a beanbag onto the grid, have the player use the number the bag falls on to fill in the next blank on the team's multiplication sheet.

Sample score sheet:

8 × _____ =

9 × _____ =

4 × _____ =

4. After putting the number in the blank, direct each player to return to his or her team by walking the length of a balance beam placed away from the groups.

5. When the team has completed all of the blanks, players perform the math operations as a team, and check their work.

Sample Variations

O – Use other math operations.

M – Create other movement opportunities.

OR – Have teams facing all sides of the grid.

O, L – Have each player toss two beanbags per turn. The *difference between* or *product of* the two numbers goes in the blank on the sheet.

OR, L – Increase or decrease the distance from the grid the students have to throw the beanbags.

OR, M – Have students dribble a ball around some cones before they arrive at the beanbag tossing area.

O – Give each student his or her own individually designed math chart to fill in.

Dicey Math

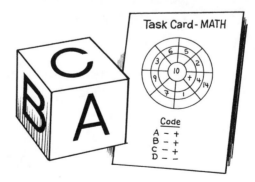

Equipment

large block or box (the die) with letters A, B, C, D on sides, use two letters twice; task card (see diagram)

Description

1. Show students a die, explaining that the letter showing on top of the die corresponds to a code at the bottom of the task card and indicates which operation to use on a problem (see example of an already completed problem in the diagram).
2. Have students take turns rolling the die.
3. After each toss of the die, students select a problem on their task sheet to solve.

Sample Variations

L – Alter the center number (e.g., rather than 10, it might become your age, 164, last 4 digits of your phone number).

L – Alter the outer number (e.g., rather than 4, it might become 26, or 17 3/8, or 14.1).

O – Alter the code that corresponds to an operation (e.g., + + + – might be replaced with + – + – or + × ÷).

L – Only require certain students to complete five of the eight problems.

OR – Have students perform the dice activity as part of the relay.

O – Individualize each student's recording sheet to accommodate his or her math ability.

Story Relays

Equipment

identical sets of word cards, listing nouns, verbs, adjectives, and other parts of speech necessary to form complete sentences equal to the number of groups (Ask the classroom teacher to help you choose appropriate words.)

Description

1. Divide the group into smaller groups of three or four students and have them line up relay style.
2. One at a time, have one player from each team run to their team's word cards.
3. Direct each player to select a word that fits (in proper sequence) into the sentence being constructed by her or his team. (Each player must add a word.)
4. Then have the player transport the card to a wall or chalkboard by balancing the card on his or her head.
5. At the wall or chalkboard, tell the player to add the card to his or her team's growing sentence.
6. Then have the player run back to the next teammate in line.

Sample Variations

M – Have runners travel to the wall through an obstacle course.

M – Rather than balance a card on their heads, have students carry the word cards between their knees or in some other unusual way.

OR – Form a single team, but have two players at a time run to the word pile to each select a word. Group decides which word will be included in the growing sentence (or story or poem).

L – Same as previous variation, but impose a time limit.

L – Create rhyming poems, limericks, or stories with a designated theme.

M – On the back of each word card, designate a movement for traveling to the wall.

L, M, – Have partners from each group move together in three-legged
OR   fashion.

L, M – Have partners from each group move together. Don't allow either to speak, and only permit one to read the reverse side of the word card that dictates the movement. That player must convey nonverbally to the partner how to move.

L – Have players alternate in a manner whereby each team is constructing its own sentence (or story) but is also adding its sentence to the other group's story.

O, L – Using a chalkboard, direct players to simply add words to sentences, rather than selecting words from piles. Require that certain words be in the sentence (from class spelling list, parts of speech study) or that sentences ask a question (that the other team must answer).

Parts of Speech

Equipment

hula hoops, jump ropes, paragraph stories, pencils or markers

Description

1. Print one paragraph per team from a previously read story on an 8 1/2 by 11 sheet of paper and tape the paper on a wall some distance from each team.

2. Within each team, designate players as either nouns, adjectives, or adverbs. You choose—simply have teams of three to five players.

3. Give a start signal, directing the first player from each team to go to the paragraph paper by jumping rope, read the paragraph, find an example of his or her part of speech, circle it, and code it (n = noun, adj = adjective, v = verb).

4. Have the player jump rope back to the team, tag the next player, and go to the end of the line and jump into and out of a hula hoop five times.

5. Play for four minutes.

6. Work with the class to correct the papers at the end of the game.

Sample Variations

O – Use other parts of speech (e.g., adverbs, prepositions).

M – Add other movements.

OR – Vary distances traveled and organizational patterns.

O – Introduce foreign language vocabulary.

O, OR – Work with the classroom teacher to group players by ability and match the level of paragraph difficulty to each group.

O – Have each player write his or her own paragraph in the regular classroom ahead of time.

Sounds the Same to Me

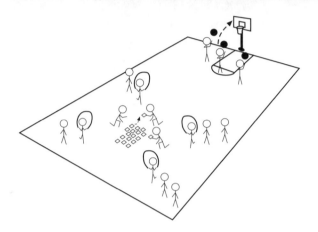

Equipment

jump ropes, basketballs, shooting area, homonym cards

Description

1. Divide the class into teams of 5 to 10.
2. Arrange the teams like the spokes of a wheel, placing the homonym cards scattered face up in the center of the pattern.
3. Signal the first player in each line to jump rope six jumps, then move to secure an accurate homonym pair (e.g., horse, hoarse).
4. Upon locating a pair, have the player move to the basketball shooting area and take one opportunity to score a basket (which equals one point).
5. Then direct the player to return to the team. The next player in line may start his turn after the first player moves to the shooting area.
6. When all pairs of cards are picked up or when three minutes are up (whichever is first), the game is over. Team members count the number of pairs and add the number of baskets. The highest total wins.
7. Play as many rounds as desired.

Sample Variations

OR – Increase the number of teams, thus decreasing waiting time.

M – Perform other movements.

OR – Play the game with partners.

L – Make this a total point game.

O – Use synonyms instead.

OR – Place all the cards face down.

Dicey Reading

Task Card - Reading
Fill in the ____vowel____, then
create the words.

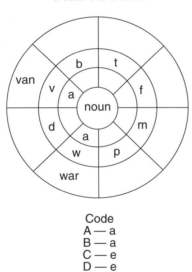

Code
A — a
B — a
C — e
D — e

Equipment

large block or box (the die) with letters A, B, C, D on sides; task card (see diagram)

Description

The format of this game is similar to Dicey Math described earlier.

1. Explain the letter showing on top of the die corresponds to a code at the bottom of the task card. The code indicates what letter(s) the student

must include in the word problem (see example of an already completed problem in the diagram).

2. Have students take turns rolling the die for the entire group.

3. After each toss of the die, direct students to select a problem on the task sheet to solve.

Sample Variations

L – Alter the center word (e.g., rather than noun, it might become verb, adjective, adverb, past tense verb).

L – Alter the outer letter (e.g., rather than "m" it might become "ta" or "fr").

L – Require that the outer letter be at the end, rather than at the beginning of a word.

L – Alter the code that corresponds to letter(s) that must be included in the word (e.g., **a a e e** might be replaced with **a e o u**, or long vowels **a e o u**, or digraphs such as **ie**, **oe**, **ue**, and **ai**).

L – Only require certain students to complete five of the eight problems.

L – Have students incorporate new words into a story or poem.

O – Individualize each student's recording sheet to accommodate his or her reading ability.

Chapter 7

International Games

A major reason for promoting international games in a curriculum is to teach children about other peoples and cultures. When played in an atmosphere of fun and good fellowship, multicultural games may be a means of broadening players' horizons, deepening their insights, and expanding their feelings of affinity for people of different cultures. Indeed, after playing various international games, players often discover that people from other cultures are not so strange after all, not so mysterious, and often not even so very far away.

To illustrate, Tchouk Ball (pronounced "chalk" ball) is a game that, like many games, is fast-paced and involves throwing, shooting, catching, and positioning. Unlike most games, however, Tchouk Ball is a game without defense or body contact, in which everyone participates and everyone is important; there are no stars. Everyone shoots during the game—and frequently. By being in the best possible field position, everyone is equally responsible for preventing the opponent from scoring. It is a mixed-skill, nonaggressive game that promotes nonthreatening participation by all individuals, irrespective of age or ability. Hence, respect toward differences in skill and one another's contributions are key game elements which, in turn, foster specific values.

In addition, the 11 other games in this chapter will expose your students to many other cultures. Enjoy this game trip around the world!

Korfball (Netherlands)

Equipment

1 basketball, baskets without backboards (about 11 feet high) or 33-gallon trash cans placed in center circle of basketball court

Description

Designed as a game that "boys and girls could play together," this activity involves running, jumping, passing, and catching. Divide a standard basketball court into two sections: the attacking zone and the defending zone. The baskets stand well within the field of play.

1. Divide the group into teams of four, two girls and two boys on each team.

2. Explain the following to the players:

   a. Players may only guard players of their own gender.

   b. After every two goals, the defenders must move to the other half of the pitch, or section. This allows for all to have an equal opportunity to play both sections of the field.

   c. No individual drives toward the basket (either by dribbling or running with the ball) are allowed; instead, players must move the ball by passing. In order to receive a pass, yet evade guards, players must do a lot of running.

   d. No kicking the ball or body contact with an opponent allowed.

   e. There must be cooperation among teammates so as to create a free shooting opportunity.

   f. No attempting to score when in a guarded position allowed (thus decreasing the importance of height). In other words, the offensive player cannot take a shot if the defender is closer to the basket than the shooter and is attempting to block the path of the shot.

g. Any infraction of these rules results in a "free pass" (no one can guard the receiver or the passer) for the other team at the point of the foul.

Sample Variations

OR – Increase the number of players per team.

L – Mandate the number of passes a team must make before taking a shot at the basket, increasing the challenge by requiring progressively more passes.

L, OR – Designate areas on the court that have higher or lower point totals if the basket is made from that region of the court.

O – Put two balls in play at the same time.

O – Change the type of ball; consider using a gator ball.

L – When the game gets to a certain point total, declare the game over and record how long it took the teams to reach that total.

L, M – Build in dribbling the ball.

L – Require passes to occur in a set time frame.

Kwik Cricket (England)

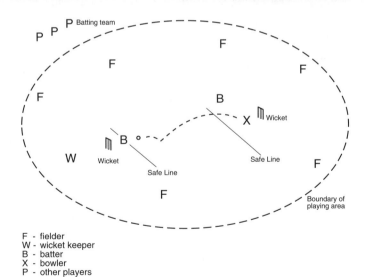

F - fielder
W - wicket keeper
B - batter
X - bowler
P - other players

Equipment

1 cricket bat (junior-size), 1 pair of wickets (2 sets of 3 short wooden poles), 1 softball, safety equipment (at teacher discretion)

Description

Played by two teams (typically 6 to 12 players each), the batting side tries to score runs, while the bowling and fielding side tries to dismiss the batters. Unlike regulation cricket, the version here (also called Kanga Ball) is easy to learn and organize. As an additional plus, a game takes only about 30 minutes.

1. To set up the play area, place wickets in the center, facing each other, about eight adult paces apart.

2. Place the batting team in order, choose a bowler (pitcher), and spread out the fielders. One fielder (the catcher or wicket-keeper) plays behind the wicket opposite the bowler to catch and throw back any missed pitches.

3. Explain the rules to the players:

   a. When at bat, the batter stands in front of one wicket and tries to hit balls thrown by the bowler, who stands at the other wicket.

   b. Pitches may be under- or overhand, but the ball should bounce once before it reaches the batter.

   c. There are no strikes or fouls, but each player's turn at bat is restricted to six pitches.

   d. There is no foul area; batters can hit in any direction.

   e. Every time the batter hits the ball he or she runs around the opposite wicket and back.

   f. The bowler keeps bowling (i.e., throws at the wicket) as soon as the ball is returned to her or him by the fielders. One run is scored if the batter returns to the wicket by running past the poles without being out.

   g. A batter is out if a bowled ball hits the wicket (any of the three poles or the stand) or if the ball is caught from a hit. If a batter is out, she or he is replaced immediately by the next batter. Teams change over when every member of the batting team has been put out.

Sample Variations

L – A fielder can put a batter out by fielding the ball and throwing it so that either (1) he or she hits the wicket before the batter can run past it or (2) it is caught by the bowler (or catcher) who hits the wicket with ball in hand before the batter can run past it.

L – When batters hit the ball, they don't have to run if they don't want to. They can choose to wait for a better pitch.

O, L – Pair batters, and allow each pair 12 pitches. One batter stands at each wicket. Only one batter at a time hits the ball, but they both carry their bats when running and must work together to score runs.

Runs are scored by batters simultaneously running either clockwise or counterclockwise (to avoid colliding with each other) between each set of wickets. Both batters must make their ground safely for *one* run to be scored, but they are not limited to one run (they score a run each time they successfully run back and forth).

L – If a batter whacks the ball out of the playing area, she or he scores six runs. If the ball touches the ground in the playing area, he or she scores four runs.

L, M – The bowler must throw underhand, but can throw on the bounce or the fly.

L – Call any pitch that cannot be reached by the batter or passes above the batter's shoulder a "wide" and count it as one run.

L – Depending on players' abilities, increase or decrease the size of the playing area.

O, L – Place rubber discs (one for each fielder) strategically in the playing area. Fielders must be in contact with their disc until the bowler releases the pitch. Batters must run every time the ball is hit.

L, OR, PL – Have four batters at one time, two at each wicket. When the ball is hit, two batters run as a pair, while the other two each run to a separate "station" and then back to their respective wickets. To increase the challenge, have the two additional batters complete a designated task at the station to score additional points.

Bocce (Italy)

Equipment

2-4 balls (sometimes called "bowls") for each player or team (small, plastic or wooden balls similar to croquet balls), one target ball or jack (another croquet ball or a tennis ball), any grassy play area

Description

Basic principles are similar to four other "national" games: American horseshoes, Scottish curling, British lawn bowls, and French jeu de boules also called *petanque*; that is, to get the balls (or boules or horseshoes) closer to the target ball (or jack or post) than the opposition.

1. Divide the group into pairs of teams of one to four players.

2. Explain that the goal is to roll, bounce, lob, or ricochet the bowls so as to have as many as possible come to rest closer to the jack than do any of the opponent's bowls.

3. Explain the rules to the players:

Examples of points scored

White scores one point.

White scores two points.

White scores three points.

a. Players decide who goes first, and that person delivers the jack and has the first turn throwing.

b. If one-person teams are playing, each player has four bowls (frequently black for one player, red for the other). Players then throw alternately, with the round ending when all eight bowls have been thrown.

c. Only one person or team scores after each round: one point is scored for each bowl nearer to the jack than the opponent's best bowl. Whichever team (or person) has the ball that is closest to the jack scores one point, regardless of who placed the jack. Thus, after the eight bowls are delivered, players walk to the other end of the playing area, tally their scores, retrieve their bowls and jack, then deliver the jack and throw the bowls again. If two opposing balls are equidistant from the jack, each cancels out the other.

d. There is no penalty for hitting an opponent's ball and moving it; in fact, this can be a good strategy.

e. After counting the score, players change ends (i.e., play back in the direction of the first throw), and the winner of the previous end throws the jack and the first ball.

f. Play to 21 points.

Sample Variations

O, L – Have players all throw from the same location (e.g., inside a hula hoop, on a beanbag, behind a throwing line) and consider a ball dead if it travels more than four feet past the jack.

O, M – Use a croquet mallet to deliver balls.

L – Permit higher-skilled players fewer throws (i.e., fewer balls).

L – In a large area, allow play to continue in various directions rather than back and forth.

L – Different colored balls score different points (e.g., the highly skilled team uses red balls, which only score single points, whereas the team using yellow balls is awarded two points for each closer ball).

L – Assign roles for four-member teams: lead delivers the jack, second scores, third measures disputed scores, fourth is team captain.

O – Play on virtually any surface that is relatively flat and obstacle-free (e.g., lawn, gravel, driveway, beach).

L – Change the order of play: In order, each player bowls one ball toward the jack. The subsequent order of play is as follows: The player or team not closest to the jack continues to bowl in succession until either (a) it succeeds in placing a ball closer than the opponent's or (b) it uses up all its balls trying to do so. (Thus, it is possible for team A, for instance, to bowl its first ball very close—touching the jack, perhaps—and then for team B to use up all of its balls trying to do better, leaving team A relative freedom for bowling its remaining balls to complete that round. In other words, team A already has one point, but can get additional points if they bowl remaining balls inside team B's failed attempt to get inside team A's first bowl.)

Tchouk Ball (Switzerland)

Equipment

1 playground ball, 2 rebound nets (can use pitch-backs), large playing area (e.g., basketball court)

Description

1. Explain the rules to students as follows:

   a. Six players from each team may be on the court at one time.

   b. To score, a player must throw the ball at the rebound net. If an opponent does not catch the rebound in the air before it has bounced, the throwing team scores a point.

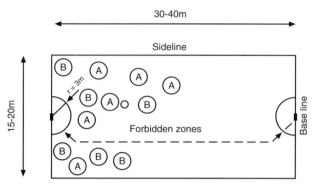

Note: These dimensions are for official matches and are only recommended for general play. You have the freedom to vary the dimensions of the field of play to suit the terrain, number of players, and degree of exertion possible and desired.

    c. No defense is permitted, that is, no intercepting or stealing a ball, blocking a throw, or hindering the progress of the opponent in any way. The only strategy for combating the opponent's attack is to position oneself to prevent the opposing team from placing a shot into an unprotected playing area.

    d. Advance the ball only by passing—no dribbling. If a team needs more than three passes they lose possession of the ball.

    e. Either team may score at either rebound net.

    f. There is a "forbidden zone" in front of the rebound net. Players holding the ball may not come into this zone, and the ball may not touch the zone before or after it has hit the rebound net (if this occurs, the opposing team earns a point).

    g. Three is a common number used for many rules in Tchouk Ball, for example, players may take no more than three steps while moving with the ball, nor hold it for more than three seconds, before they must throw it to a teammate or shoot it at the net; the same net may be attacked no more than three consecutive times by each team.

2. Explain scoring details as follows:

    a. Team in possession earns a point when its shot, on being returned by the rebound net, is not caught by the opposing side before it bounces. The opposing team restarts play.

    b. When the ball bounces back into the forbidden zone or a shot at the net hits this area, the opposing team earns a point.

    c. When the team in possession's shot misses the rebound net, the opposing team earns a point.

    d. When the team in possession rebounds the ball causing it to fall outside the boundary lines, the opposing team earns a point.

e. When a player shoots at the net and the ball bounces back to her- or himself, the opposing team earns a point.

Sample Variations

O, L – If the play area is limited, use only one rebound net for two teams, changing from a two-way to a one-way game.

L – Alter the dimensions of the playing field or the forbidden zone (a smaller zone may be more compatible with lower skill levels).

L, M, PL – Increase the number of players, while either decreasing the number of steps allowed or perhaps requiring the ball to be dribbled after holding it for three seconds.

O – Use a different ball (a team handball is closest to the official ball used in Taiwan).

O – Play on another surface (e.g., turf, playground, gymnasium).

L – Allow players to drop the ball without penalty after receiving a pass.

L – Award different point values to different locations on the court.

L – Allow dribbling.

Tapu-Ae (New Zealand)

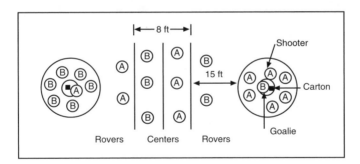

Equipment

2 different-colored playground balls, 2 milk cartons

Description

1. Divide the group into two equal teams.

2. Designate players to fill the following positions on each team: three centers, one goalie, two or more shooters, and two or more rovers. It also is desirable to assign one scorer and two referees to keep an accurate score.

3. To begin, have players assume positions as shown in the diagram. Direct a center from each team to hold a ball. The teacher determines the size of the shooting circles, goalie circles, and field size.

4. Signal the centers to attempt to throw to the shooters on their respective teams.

5. Have the receiving shooters attempt to knock over the carton with the ball.

6. Meanwhile, goalies protect their respective cartons, and they and the rovers attempt to intercept the ball and pass it to their own team-mates.

7. Explain that the ball must go to one of the centers while being passed across to the opposite court. Both balls may be in one circle at the same time, making it more difficult for the goalie to protect the carton.

8. After a given number of points, direct players to rotate positions.

9. In addition, explain the following rules:

   a. Each type of player must remain within her or his own area.

   b. You may not run with the ball.

   c. You must pass the ball within five seconds.

   d. In case of a rule infringement, the ball goes to the other team.

   e. Your team earns one point for scoring with your team's own ball and two points for scoring with your opponent's ball.

Sample Variations

O – Use basketballs, soccer balls, or Nerf balls and 10 pins or small traffic cones.

L, M, – Designate certain rovers as allowed to run with the ball, while others
PU   must hand dribble the ball.

O – Modify the size of one or both circle diameters and one or both center widths.

L – Require rovers or centers to pass to at least one other rover or center before their team can pass to their own shooters; require the same from shooters before their team can attempt to score.

L – Designate a rover to rove into the opponent's territory.

L – Allow three steps before a player passes the ball.

O – Increase the number of cartons a goalie must guard.

L – Do not allow goalies to use their hands to protect the cartons.

'Ulu Maika (Hawaii)

Equipment
playground balls, gallon milk cartons

Description
You can play this game a couple of ways. First, see who can roll the ball the farthest for the greatest distance, using an underhand bowling motion. Second, roll the ball between two gallon milk cartons placed 30 to 50 feet away from the rolling start line.

Explain the rules to the students:

1. You may only roll the ball; no bouncing.

2. In the distance version, you may roll the ball three times and add total yardage to get your final score.

3. In the other version, you earn two points for every ball you send through the milk cartons without touching them. But you must deduct one point for each milk carton the ball touches per roll. You get three rolling attempts for a total score.

Sample Variations
O – Increase the size of the playground ball and the distance between the roller and the cartons.

O – Play on a different surface (e.g., grass).

O – Decrease the width between the cartons.

O – Place a rope in the field over which the ball must fly, then let it roll for distance.

O – Allow students to roll more than one ball per roll, challenging movement control.

L – Add a team's total distance scores and challenge another team's total score.

L – Create teams of three, four, or five players and alternate the nature of the throws (overhand, underhand, or sidearm) by the team members, then total up the distance for the entire team. See if they can beat their total next time.

L – Award different point totals for the different distances away the roller is from the cartons, e.g., one point for 20 feet, two points for 30 feet, and so on.

L – Award different points for successfully rolling a ball through different widths of the carton placements.

One, Two, Three Dragon (Japan)

Equipment

Description

1. Form groups of approximately 10 players per team.
2. Ask each team to form a line, placing their hands on the shoulders of the person standing in front of them. The first person becomes the dragon's head, the last person, the dragon's tail.
3. To begin, the tail calls out "one, two, three dragon."
4. The head starts to run, trying to catch its own tail without anyone letting go of the person they are connected to.
5. If the line (body) "breaks," the head becomes the tail, and the next person in line becomes the head.

6. Play for 45-second intervals and then rotate everyone up to the next position.

7. Score one point if the head catches the tail before the time limit is up. If the head can't catch the tail before the time limit is up, score a point for the tail.

Sample Variations

M, PU – Use another movement form, such as skipping.

    L – Change the size of the playing area.

    PL – Alter the speed of the game by forming teams of 6 or 12 or more.

    L – Have players hold on to the person in front of them with one hand instead of two.

    L – Play for more than 45 seconds at a time.

Chapete (Mexico)

Equipment

1 gator or Nerf ball per small group

Description

1. Arrange no more than eight players in a circle. Make sure they aren't too close to one another (about arm's-length apart).

2. Direct one player to begin the game by tossing the ball up into the air toward another player, who in turn passes the ball to another player using one of his or her body parts, for example, an elbow, a knee, or a hip (neither heads nor hands are allowed).

3. Time the action.

4. If the ball hits the ground, start over again.

5. Set two minutes as the time challenge for each group to meet.

Sample Variations

PL – Reduce or increase the number of players per team.

OR – Increase the distance between each player.

L, M – Only allow players to use body parts waist-level and below or waist-to shoulder-level.

M – Tell players to allow the ball to bounce first, then use a body part to pass it to another teammate.

L – Keep score, awarding one point for every successful pass.

L – Introduce some math concepts such as percentages by playing the game for three minutes, recording the time the ball is kept off of the ground, and finding the percentage of air time to total time. Use this percentage as the scoring mechanism (e.g., 52 % air time scores 52 points that round).

L – Award one point for every pass that was receivable and one additional point for every pass that was successfully completed.

Hoops (Greece)

Equipment

1 hula hoop and 1 playground ball per player

Description

1. Divide the group into teams of 5 to 10 and give each team one hula hoop and one ball per player.

2. Have each team select one player to be the hoop roller while the other players move 30 to 40 feet away.

3. Tell the hoop roller to roll the hoop toward his or her teammates. Teammates can be on either side of the hoop.

4. As the hoop passes by, direct the team members to toss their playground balls through the hoop without touching the hoop or knocking it down. The round ends if a ball or player touches the hoop or when the hoop stops rolling on its own. Keep retrieving and passing the balls through the hoop as long as the hoop is rolling. Score one point for every ball passing through the hoop.

5. Explain that the team with the most balls through the hoop before the hoop stops rolling wins that round.

6. Play as many rounds as desired.

Sample Variations

OR – Organize the ball throwers so they have to remain on the same side of the rolling hoop.

OR – Create teams of three, one hoop roller and two ball throwers.

O – Try using beanbags instead of balls.

O – Use gator balls only and direct the throwers to bounce the ball through the hoop.

O – Add another hoop per team.

OR, L – Make the game more difficult by maintaining a certain distance the ball throwers must be from the hoop.

M, PU – Direct players to dribble the ball as they chase after the hoop.

L – Play for prescribed time (45 seconds or so) or a prescribed distance on a field, allowing teams to roll the hoop as many times as needed.

L – Score points based on the difficulty of the throw.

PL, OR – Play with fewer players on each team.

M – Ask players to throw with their nonpreferred arms, behind their backs, through their legs, or with two bounces.

Hop Race (Native American)

Equipment

1 milk carton per team

Description

1. Divide the group into multiple teams of no more than five per team.
2. Have each team form a line, at least 15 feet from a milk carton.
3. Explain that the object of the race is to see how many turns each team can take in one minute.
4. Direct one player at a time from each team to hop down and around that team's milk carton, down on the right foot, back on the left foot.
5. Send the next player hopping around the milk carton when the first player tags him or her, and so on through the team.
6. Signal players to stop when one minute has passed.
7. Play as many rounds as desired.
8. Have teams find the total number of turns their players took at the end of play.

Sample Variations

OR – Allow two players at a time from each team to travel around the cartons.

OR – Line up the players on each team in a shuttle pattern or as spokes in a wheel.

L – Increase the amount of playing time, record the score, and challenge students to beat it next time.

M, OR – Place obstacles in the path of the players that they have to go over, around, or under.

OR – Challenge another class after recording your total class time.

M – Designate hopping styles.

OR, PL – Assign fewer players per team.

Lame Chicken (China)

Equipment

10 lummi sticks per group

Description

1. Divide the class into groups of two or more players each.

2. For each group, spread 10 lummi sticks on the ground, about one foot apart from one another in an even row.

3. Explain how to play:

   a. The first player gets to hop over the sticks without touching or moving any of the sticks.

   b. Upon successfully hopping over the 10 sticks, the player must lean over and pick up the 10th stick and then return across the remaining sticks, again by hopping over them.

   c. Continue playing until all the remaining sticks are picked up, until the player's nonhopping foot touches the ground (only hopping on the same foot is allowed), or until the player touches one of the sticks lying on the ground.

   d. Replace the 10 lummi sticks, and have the next player attempt to see how many sticks he or she can pick up.

Sample Variations

O – Use jump ropes instead of sticks.

OR – Increase the distance between the sticks.

L, M – Ask players to jump with two feet together instead of hopping.

L, M – Time the travel across the sticks to see who can successfully complete the task the fastest.

O, L, PL – Have partners move together across the sticks and ask them to pick up newspaper balls placed next to each stick.

O, P, L – Physically connect players to one another (holding hands) and direct them to move together across ropes.

M, L – Change the locomotor movement required for each direction across the lummi sticks.

O – Use more or fewer sticks per game.

Bounce Eye (Australia)

Equipment

3 partially deflated playground balls per student, marking paint or jump ropes

Description

1. Create a circle on a grassy area (if available), approximately three feet in diameter, using marking paint or a long jump rope tied together, one circle per every six students.
2. Have students stand 10 to 15 feet away from their group's circle.
3. Give each student one playground ball, and place two balls per student inside the circle.
4. Have each student take a turn, throwing, rolling, and bouncing (student choice) a ball into the circle. Direct each player to gather all the balls that leave the circle during his turn. If no ball leaves the circle upon a rolling attempt, that player must watch the rest of the game.
5. Continue playing until the circle is empty. Try to reduce the time it takes to empty the circle of balls.
6. Play as many rounds as desired.

Sample Variations

O – Use inflated balls.

O – Use Nerf or gator balls or partially deflated footballs.

L – Score a point for every ball you have at the end of the game.

L – See how much time it takes to knock all the balls out of the circle.

L, M – Have players roll the ball through their legs while standing with their backs to the circle.

OR, PL – Add more players to each circle.

OR, PL – Play with only three players per circle—look out, this is a fast game.

L, PL – Have players roll the ball while others retrieve, taking turns in these roles.

Chapter 8

Old Favorites . . . and More

As discussed in part I, the traditional forms of a few of the activities in this chapter have been criticized by some as unsuitable for inclusion in today's curriculum. Many of the criticisms are quite legitimate. Indeed, a game that permits physical activity for only one or two players, singles out individuals for failure, or is developmentally inappropriate deserves scrutiny. We continue to argue, however, that examining and sometimes changing these activities might be preferable to simply dismissing them. Thus, we present the games (e.g., kickball, relay races, and line soccer) that have been assigned to the "Physical Education Hall of Shame," explaining the shameful attributes of their traditional forms. Then we suggest a few alternatives (kickball becomes Maple Hill Ball, relay races become Couples Races, and line soccer becomes Maligned Soccer); we have designed the alternatives to correct or minimize each game's alleged deficiencies as well as accentuate or increase its positive features and potential. In their altered forms, we believe these games to be every bit as good as the other old favorites from the first edition that we have included here.

We offer these games for you to share with the next generation of students, knowing you're now well-prepared to modify them to best suit the needs and interests of your students in your situation. Have fun!

Couples Races (Relay Race Variations)

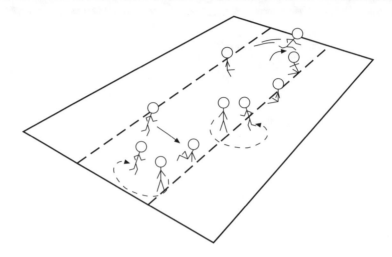

A concern with traditional relays is that (1) they take too long to set up, explain, actually run, and then calm students down before continuing to the next activity, (2) each player is inactive during most of the relay, and (3) students perform in front of most of the class "who have little else to do but watch and make fun of their classmates' mistakes" (Williams, 1992). Merits include enabling students to practice skills and teamwork as they follow instructions. In addition, many students enjoy them.

Equipment

none initially, but all small equipment can be used, if desired (e.g., balls, ropes, hoops)

Description

1. Have partners form two lines, 20 feet apart, facing one another.
2. Give one line of participants instructions to perform several tasks in sequence.
3. Make each player in the other line responsible for supporting his or her own partner in correctly completing the sequenced tasks. For example, say, "Run around your partner, touch an elbow to a knee, and then jump over your partner. I'll know the race is over when you've all returned to the starting line and *everyone* is sitting down. Partner watching, make sure your partner does everything and in the right order."

Sample Variations

M – Vary the number of tasks (only two tasks or as many as six).

L – Alter the amount or specificity of information (e.g., "Touch a wall" versus "Locate two adjacent walls and touch each simultaneously with your nose").

L – Permit players to choose the order in which they will perform the designated tasks (perhaps in brief collaboration with their partners). Note how little opportunity there is for most of the class to make fun of a few now.

M, O – Suggest four tasks from which the players must select three and then add one of their own (again, perhaps in collaboration with their partners).

M, L – Include tasks that require interacting with several players in addition to their own partners (e.g., shuttlecock must be passed back and forth six times with each of the two other players from the other line [one may be your own partner]).

OR – Form four lines, not two. The two moving lines must avoid colliding with one another. Or require them to exchange equipment somehow (e.g., passing and catching, juggling).

M – Have players manipulate balls and ropes.

Maple Hill Ball (Kickball Variations)

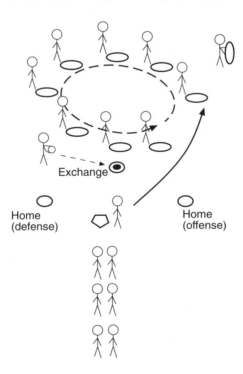

The main concern with traditional kickball is that too many players are uninvolved. Its merits include that it reinforces many aspects of other activities, such as baseball and soccer, and students generally seem to enjoy playing.

Equipment

11 hula hoops, 4 different-size playground balls, 3 jump ropes, 2 milk cartons, 2 lummi sticks, 1 two-inch-wide band cut from an old inner tube

Description

1. Divide the group into two teams, 8 to 15 players each of mixed abilities.
2. Further divide the offense into five subgroups.
3. Have the defense scatter randomly in the play area.
4. Explain the offensive roles and rules as follows:

   a. One subgroup at a time is at bat.

   b. After kicking successfully, the kicker runs to jump rope and jumps with it 12 times while other group members move through a hoop held vertically by another member of the kicking subgroup in the outfield (see diagram).

   c. Then all group members return to home base.

   d. Turn limit (not time limit): each subgroup gets one turn, then all play defense.

5. Explain the defensive roles and rules as follows:

   a. Start outside hoops; as ball is kicked, one defensive player retrieves the ball and the other defensive players run to a hoop (one per hoop).

   b. The defensive player with the ball passes it to a team member inside his or her hoop, who passes to another teammate inside a hoop and so on until all players inside hoops have received the ball.

   c. Last player to receive ball runs to another hoop, exchanges the ball kicked and thrown for another ball, takes the new ball to the defense's home base (another hoop). If the ball reaches home base before all offensive players return to home base, runs do not count.

Sample Variations

Try changing the defense in the following ways:

   O – Reduce the number of hoops to one less than the number of defensive players; only one hoop may be shared.

   O, L – Exchange one ball for three.

   O, L – Balance a lummi stick across two cartons.

L – Reduce distance between ball exchange areas, *but* require last player to put band around knees before running to exchange balls.

Try changing the offense in the following ways:

L, M – Require each member of group to jump rope and go through hoop.

L, M – Have all run at same time; each must do two of the following:

a. Jump rope 15 times.

b. Roll hoop and dive through before it falls.

c. With three team members, run to milk carton, and either build a human pyramid or complete two sets of leapfrog.

L, PU – Have players select their own subgroups of three or four. One of these kicks the pitched ball; however, prior to doing so, each of them must select one of several tasks they'll perform once the ball is kicked. To vary the level of challenge, it helps to list task choices that progress in degree of difficulty. For instance, do the following:

a. Kick a ball through two cartons placed five feet apart, without knocking either carton down.

b. Kick a ball at two cartons placed three feet apart, and knock one of them down.

c. Kick a ball through two cartons placed three feet apart, without knocking either carton down.

d. Dribble a ball through four cartons placed three feet apart, without knocking any of them down.

M – Have everyone on the offensive team perform a task specific to his or her individual needs.

M – Design other tasks for the batters to perform besides bowling.

Maple Hill—Hit and Run

Equipment

1 batting tee, hoops (one less than number of fielders), different types of balls, lummi sticks, milk cartons, 1 jump rope

Description

1. Divide the group into two teams of 8-15 players per team.

2. Explain the roles and rules as follows:

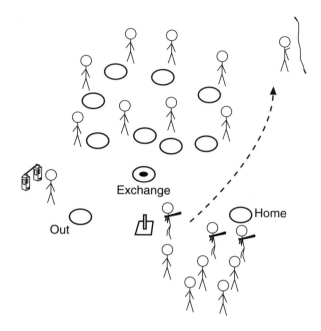

a. Batters: Divide team members into three groups. Each group gets to have one batting turn per inning (alternate the player who bats). The batter strikes the ball and, together with the rest of the players in the group, runs to the jump rope stretched out on the floor (placed 50 to 100 feet away in right field). The group members must jump over the rope 10 times, and then all must return to the home hoop as fast as possible.

b. Fielders: Begin outside the hoops, and one player fields the batted ball. The rest of the fielders stand inside their hoops. Throw the ball among eight different players, and the last player to receive a throw runs to the exchange hoop and exchanges the batted ball with another one. That player next must balance a lummi stick across two milk cartons. Then he or she runs to the out hoop and places the ball inside it. If batters return to the home hoop before the fielders complete their tasks, then they score one run.

c. This is a turn-limit game (each batting group gets one turn at bat per inning).

Sample Variations

L – Have the fielding team line up in a column; the person retrieving the ball must crawl under the other fielders.

O – Place six to eight bases in a semicircle that batters must run around.

O – Vary the size, shape, and color of the balls.

M, PU – Assign fielders and batters other tasks or let them choose from harder and easier tasks, earning points based on D of D.

L – Allow the fielders to take runs away from the batters by picking up three extra balls from the exchange hoop. (Subtract the number of extra balls successfully placed in the exchange hoop from the batters' score.)

Maligned Soccer (Line Soccer Variations)

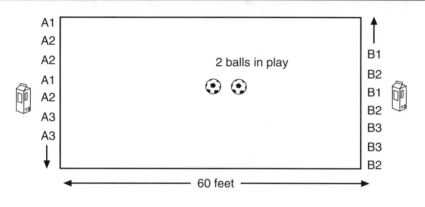

Teacher

Concerns with traditional line soccer are (1) minimal participation time, (2) putting students on display in front of their peers, and (3) skilled players possibly controlling the ball and kicking it toward a less-skilled opponent. But it enhances soccer skills and is fast-paced and exciting.

Equipment

several soccer balls, hula hoops, cartons or cones

Description

Maligned Soccer is the same as traditional line soccer except for the following:

1. Assign several players on each team the same number.

2. Put two balls in play.

3. The teacher calls out one or more numbers and those players attempt to score while the remaining players on line defend their cartons.

4. Score only when an opponent knocks down a carton, which is placed behind a team's "line" in a location determined by that team.

Sample Variations

L – Score by kicking through a hula hoop held by a teammate.

OR – Score by kicking between two cones, behind which a teammate must stop the ball and control it.

L, OR – Create four teams (lines).

L, OR – Create four teams, but now allow the ball to pass in either direction between the two cones added in second variation.

PL, L – Have players work in pairs. Object is to score, but now opposing pairs may attempt to steal the ball.

L – Involve all players simultaneously now instead of calling numbers. First, scatter hoops about the play area. Again working in pairs, have the players try to score points against their partners: one player in each pair tries to dribble the ball from hoop to hoop, while the other player tries to steal the ball. A player scores when he or she successfully moves the ball into a hoop. After scoring, the player turns the ball over to the partner.

L – Same as previous variation, except now allow each partner to score as many points as possible in a specified time period. Allow higher-skilled players less scoring time and require them to score a specified number of goals in succession for the points to count.

One Behind

Equipment

Description

1. Explain that players must always remain one movement behind you. For example, you perform movement A (hands on hips), and players

memorize it. When you perform movement B (hands on shoulders), the players perform movement A, and so on.

2. Have players scatter at random in front of you.
3. Practice a few moves slowly, if necessary.
4. Play the game as long as desired.
5. Tap into all locomotor, nonlocomotor, and fitness movements—whatever you're currently stressing in your curriculum.

Sample Variations

M – Change the sequence of movements.

L – Increase or decrease the delay time between the movement presentation and the actual movement performance.

O – Incorporate equipment (e.g., dribble a ball, jump rope).

L – Increase the number of "behinds" to three, four, or five.

L, M, PU – Use this game for fitness development or a warm-up.

Four-Corner Relay

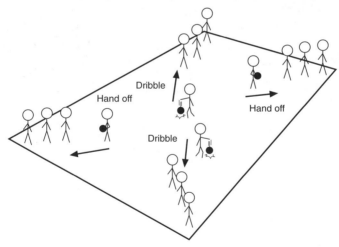

Equipment

4 balls (1 per team)

Description

1. Divide the group into four teams of about 5 to 10.
2. Have each team line up in its own corner of the gym.
3. Direct the first person from each team to dribble to the center of the gym.

4. Have each player continue diagonally to the opposite corner of the gym (all four players will crisscross one another), hand the ball off to the next player, and go to the end of the line of this new team. The player who receives the ball dribbles diagonally across the gym.

5. Explain that the first team to return all players to their original positions wins the game.

Sample Variations

L – Allow players to carry the ball.

M – Designate the height of the dribble allowed.

O – Set up cones that players must travel around.

M – Ask players to use their nonpreferred hands.

M – Work on specific dribbling skills.

M – Build in rotary motion movements.

Add-On Tag

Equipment

Description

1. Designate three ITs, and have the other players scatter at random in front of them.

2. Signal the ITs to chase the other players.

3. When tagged, have the tagged player join hands with the IT who tagged him or her, and both chase the rest of the players. When tagged, players continue to "add on" to the three growing lines. Everyone in the lines is now also IT.

4. After the last player is tagged, begin the game again with three new ITs.

Sample Variations

L – Designate fewer or more starting ITs.

L – Reduce playing area.

OR – As players add on, alternate the direction each faces, such as front, back, front, back.

L – Designate a safe area in which players may not be tagged.

L, OR – Every time IT reaches four people, have IT split into two new tagging pairs.

Octopus Tag

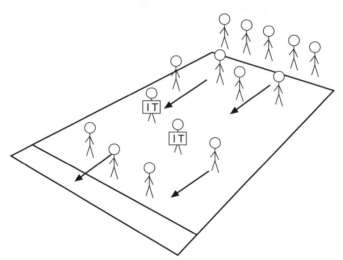

Equipment

Description

1. Designate two "octopuses" (ITs) and call the rest of the players "fish."
2. Place the two octopuses in the middle of the play area, then signal the fish to run across the playing area while the two octopuses chase the fish.
3. If a fish is tagged, explain that he or she is frozen in that spot. The immobile fish can tag the running fish, freezing them also.
4. End the game when almost everyone is caught (frozen).

Sample Variations

L – Increase the number of ITs.

L – Change the dimensions of the playing area.

L – Permit the frozen players to pivot on one foot, giving them greater range of movement.

PL – Play the game in three-legged pairs, either by having partners stand side by side or tying their inside legs together.

O – Have players use balls to tag each other.

L – Set a time limit in which the octopuses have to catch everyone.

Busy Bee

Contributed by Inge Morisbak—Norway

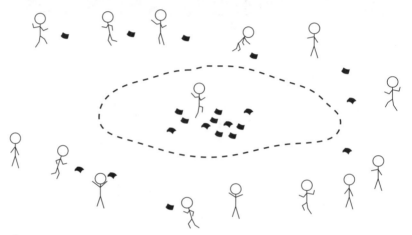

Equipment

beanbags, ropes or chalk

Description

1. Form a large circle with the ropes or chalk and place several beanbags inside it.
2. Designate one player to stand in the circle and have the rest of the players scatter around the rope circle.
3. Signal the player with all the beanbags inside the circle to start throwing them out of the circle, trying to clean out the circle completely.
4. Direct all the other players to try to catch the bags in the air and immediately return them to the circle.
5. Continue playing as long as desired.

Sample Variations

O – Change the objects used to different sizes, textures, and colors.

L – Stop the objects using body parts other than the hands (e.g., feet only).

L – Designate a specific propulsion skill players must use.

OR, PL – Place more players inside the circle.

OR – Increase or decrease the size of the circle.

M – Designate the levels players move at (e.g., crawling, kneeling, or standing).

Hit the Club

Contributed by Reidar Hagan—Norway

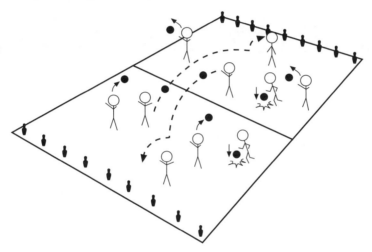

Equipment

8-10 Indian clubs or cartons, 4-6 medium-size playground balls per team

Description

1. Divide the group into two teams.

2. Have each team scatter randomly on their half of the gym.

3. Explain the rules as follows:

   a. Neither team is permitted to cross the center dividing line.

   b. Players must throw or roll the balls at the opposing team's clubs.

   c. Players may use any body part to try to stop the balls before they hit their own clubs.

4. Declare the team that has knocked over the most clubs at the end of the designated time period the winner of the round.

5. Play as many rounds as desired.

Sample Variations

P – Increase or decrease the number of players on each team.

O – Increase or decrease the number of balls used in the game.

O, L – Use milk cartons instead of Indian clubs, or mix the two, and award different numbers of points for each.

O – Use Nerf balls.

M – Have players change their levels (e.g., sitting, kneeling, or standing).

M – Have players vary the propulsion skills (e.g., kicking, striking).

Basketbowl

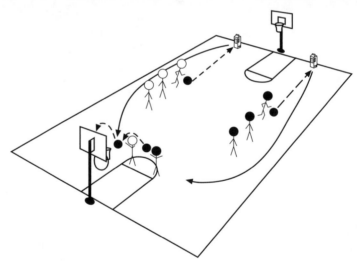

Equipment

variety of balls, hula hoops, milk cartons

Description

1. Divide group into teams of four players each.

2. Arrange teams in any relay pattern, place milk cartons on one end of the court and balls for shooting baskets at the other end, and hang a hula hoop from the basket students will shoot at.

3. Direct the first player on each team to attempt to bowl the ball and knock over a milk carton. Allow only one attempt per person.

4. Next, have the player retrieve the ball and move to the shooting area, where he or she takes one shot at the basket or the hula hoop hanging from the basket. The player then gets the rebound and moves back to his or her team and hands the ball to the next player.

5. Award two points for a basket, one for a hoop, and one for hitting a carton. The team with the most points after six minutes wins the round.

Sample Variations

O – Add more milk cartons.

L – Increase or decrease the distance between the cartons to the bowling line.

L – Change the point values.

L – Gradually introduce specific basketball rules.

L – Permit players to develop their own strategies for retrieving the ball.

O – Add a second ball to each group.

Four-Corners Volleyball

Equipment

4-8 balls per game, 2 nets

Description

1. Use the two nets to divide the playing area into four equal areas as shown in the diagram.

2. Divide the group into four teams of 6 to 10.

3. Give each team one or two balls.

4. Explain that the object of this game is for each team to get rid of all the balls in their quarter of the playing area.

5. Signal players to use their volleyball skills to get the balls into the other teams' quarters.

6. See if players can keep the balls moving for three minutes.

Sample Variations

O – Increase the number of balls.

OR – Change the position of the nets.

L – Develop a point scoring system.

O, L – Use a variety of balls and awarded points based on the difficulty of handling each type.

L – Direct everyone in a quarter to hit the ball before sending it over the net.

Lucky Seven

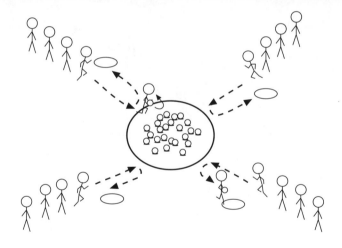

Equipment
various balls, jump ropes, hoops, cones

Description

1. Divide the group into four equal teams.
2. Line up teams in the four-corner relay pattern, each team facing another team on the diagonal, with a rope circle in the middle filled with small objects.
3. Signal the first player in each team to run out to the objects in the circle, pick one up, and return to his or her team and tag the next player in line.
4. Continue play until all the objects in the circle are gone.
5. Declare the team with the most objects the winner.

Sample Variations

M – Change the locomotor movement required.

L – Have the runner return the objects to his or her team using feet only.

M – Change the direction and level of movement required (e.g., move backward at a low level).

M – Have players weave in and out of teammates upon returning with an object before going to the end of the line.

Appendix

Task Complexity: Kicking Factors

	Easy ⟶ Difficult	
Object size	Large	Small
Foot used	Preferred	Nonpreferred
Object weight	Light	Heavy
Type of kick	Toe	Instep
Object movement	Stationary	Fast
Object shape	Round	Oblong

Task Complexity: Catching Factors

	Easy ⟶ Difficult		
Object color	Blue	Yellow	White
Angle of trajection	Horizontal	Vertical	Arc
Object size	Large	Medium	Small
Object speed	Slow	Fast	Faster
Object weight	Light	Medium	Heavy
Object texture	Soft	Firm	Hard
Distance	Near	Medium	Far
Reception location	Midline	Preferred side	Nonpreferred side

Task Complexity: Jumping Factors

	Easy → Difficult		
Type of jump	Jump down	Horizontal jump	Vertical jump
Landing surface	Crash pads	Sawdust pit Gym mat	Concrete surface
Body position	Compact		Extended

Task Complexity: Throwing Factors

	Easy → Difficult		
Object size	Small	Medium	Large
Object shape	Round	Oblong	Irregular
Pattern used	Overarm	Underarm	Sidearm
Direction	Toward a wall	Toward a target, preferred side	Toward a target, nonpreferred side
Target movement	Stationary	Slightly moving	Moving rapidly

Task Complexity: Striking Factors

	Easy → Difficult		
Object size	Large	Medium	Small
Object shape	Round	Oblong	Irregular
Angle of trajectory	Horizontal	Vertical	Arc
Reception location	Close to body	Preferred side	Nonpreferred side
Object color/background color	Blue/white	Yellow/white	White/white
Object movement	Stationary	Slow	Fast

Task Complexity: Strength Factors

	Easy		Difficult
Weight	5 lbs	10 lbs	15 lbs
Duration	5 repetitions/ 10 seconds	10 repetitions/ 20 seconds	15 repetitions/ 30 seconds
	5 repetitions/ 15 seconds	10 repetitions/ 25 seconds	15 repetitions/ 40 seconds
Distance/height	100 yards/3 feet	220 yards/6 feet	440 yards/9 feet

Task Complexity: Balance Factors

	Easy		Difficult
Size of support base	Eight body parts	Four body parts	One body part
Center of gravity (C of G)	Directly over and close to the base of support	Slightly off center and above base of support	Moderately off center and far above the base of support
Speed	Slow	Fast	Faster
Time	8 seconds	18 seconds	30 seconds

Task Complexity: Agility Factors

	Easy		Difficult
Travel distance	Run, jump one foot, continue running	Run, jump three feet, continue running	Run, jump five feet, continue running
Height	Jump over 6-inch-high object	Jump over 1-foot-high object	Jump over 1 1/2-foot-high object
Direction change	One	Two	Four
Transition rhythm	Smooth	Irregular	Rough

Task Complexity: Swinging/Swaying Factors

	Easy ⟶ Difficult		
Speed	Slow	Medium	Fast
Direction	One	Two	Three
Number of body parts	Two	Three	Four
Level	Medium	Low	High
External aids	None	One	Three

Task Complexity: Locomotor Factors–Even/Uneven-Beat Skills

	Easy ⟶ Difficult			
Level	Medium	High	Low	
Pathway	Curved	Angular	Zigzag	
Direction	Forward	Sideward	Backward	
Time	Slow	Medium	Fast	
Force	Light	Medium	Heavy	
Flow	Free	Jerky	Bound	
Relationship	Individual body within space	Child-child Child-group	Child-small equipment	Child-large equipment

Task Complexity: Locomotor Factors–Rotary Motions

	Easy ⟶ Difficult	
Rhythm	Smooth	Irregular
Number/duration	One/short	Several/long
End position	Compact	Extended
Speed	Slow	Fast
Starting position	Compact	Extended
Direction of movement	Sideward	Backward
Body posture	Compact	Extended
Body parts contacting the surface	Many	Few

References

Bloom, B. (1956). *Taxonomy of educational objectives: The classification of educational goals. Handbook I: Cognitive domain.* New York: Longmans Green.

Bunker, D., & Thorpe, R. (1982). A model for the teaching of games in secondary schools. *Bulletin of Physical Education, 18*(1), 5-8.

Bushnell, N. (1983). Foreword. In R. von Oech, *A whack on the side of the head.* New York: Warner Books.

Cratty, B. (1976). *Active learning.* Englewood Cliffs, NJ: Prentice-Hall.

Eisen, G. (1988). *Children and play in the holocaust: Games among the shadows.* Amherst, MA: University of Massachusetts Press.

Ellis, M. (1983). *Similarities and differences in games: A system for classification.* Paper presented at the AIESEP Congress, Teaching Team Sports, Rome, Italy.

Graham, G., Holt/Hale, S., & Parker, M. (1993). *Children moving: A reflective approach to teaching physical education* (3rd ed.). Palo Alto, CA: Mayfield.

Griffin, L.L., Mitchell, S.A., & Oslin, J.L. (1997). *Teaching sport concepts and skills: A tactical games approach.* Champaign, IL: Human Kinetics.

Harter, S., & Robinson, N. (1993). *The perceived directionality of the link between approval and self-worth: The liabilities of a looking glass orientation among young adolescents.* Unpublished manuscript, University of Denver, Department of Psychology, Denver.

Hoffman, H., Young, J., & Klesius, S. (1981). *Meaningful movement for children.* Boston: Allyn and Bacon.

Kirchner, G. (1992). *Physical education for elementary school children* (8th ed.). Dubuque, IA: Wm. C. Brown.

Kissler, A. (1994). *On course: Games for everyone.* Auburn, CA: On Course, Inc.

Morris, G.S.D. (1976). *How to change the games children play.* Minneapolis: Burgess.

Morris, G.S.D. (1980). *Elementary physical education: Toward inclusion.* Salt Lake City: Brighton Press.

Morris, G. S. D., & Stiehl, J. (1985). *Physical education: From intent to action.* Columbus, OH: Chas. E. Merrill.

Morris, G.S.D., & Stiehl, J. (1989). *Changing kids' games.* Champaign, IL: Human Kinetics.

Orlick, T. (1978). *The cooperative sports and games book.* New York: Pantheon.

Pangrazi, R.P., & Dauer, V.P. (1995). *Dynamic physical education for elementary school children* (11th ed.). Boston: Allyn & Bacon.

Rohnke, K., & Butler, S. (1995). *Quicksilver.* Dubuque, IA: Kendall/Hunt.

Thorpe, R., & Bunker, D. (1982). From theory to practice: Two examples of an "understanding approach" to the teaching of games. *Bulletin of Physical Education,* 18, 9-16.

Thorpe, R., Bunker, D., & Almond, L. (1984). A change in focus for the teaching of games. Paper presented at the Olympic Scientific Congress, Eugene, OR.

Turner, A. (1996). Myth or reality? *Journal of Physical Education, Recreation and Dance,* 67(4), 46-55.

Wegener, A.B. (1930). *Play games!* New York: Abingdon Press.

Weiss, M.R., McAuley, E., Ebbeck, V. and Wiese, D.M. (1990). Self esteem and causal attributions for children's physical and social competence in sport. *Journal of Sport and Exercise Psychology,* 24, 49-58.

Werner, P., & Almond, L. (1990). Models of games education. *Journal of Physical Education, Recreation and Dance,* 61(4), 23-27.

Werner, P., Thorpe, R., & Bunker, D. (1996). Teaching Games for Understanding: Evolution of a model. *Journal of Physical Education, Recreation and Dance,* 61(1), 28-33.

Williams, N.F. (1992) The physical education hall of shame. *Journal of Physical Education, Recreation and Dance,* 63(6), 57-60.

About the Authors

G.S. Don Morris (left), Jim Stiehl (right)

G.S. Don Morris, PhD, is a professor at California State Polytechnic University-Pomona, where he coordinates curriculum, instruction, and teacher education in kinesiology. Dr. Morris teaches in local elementary schools and is involved in ongoing research and intervention programs designed to enhance children's comprehensive health status. He also designed and created a model elementary PE curriculum in the Chino Unified School District. He has been a Fulbright Scholar and a Marshall Researcher. In his leisure time he enjoys snow skiing, all water activities, and the Sierra Nevada mountains.

Jim Stiehl, PhD, is a professor and the director of the School of Kinesiology and Physical Education at the University of Northern Colorado. He has more than 30 years of experience working with underserved kids and alternative programs. Dr. Stiehl received the Scholar Award from the Central District of the American Alliance for Health, Physical Education, Recreation and Dance (AAHPERD) in 1993. He also was a co-recipient of a Research Writing Award from AAHPERD in 1991, is past chair of the council on outdoor education, and is an instructor for the National Outdoor Leadership School. During his professional career, Dr. Stiehl has taught physical education, as well as elementary and special education classes. Mountaineering is his favorite leisure activity.

Related Books from Human Kinetics

More Team Building Challenges
Daniel W. Midura, MEd, and Donald R. Glover, MS
1995 • Paper • 120 pp • Item BMID0785
ISBN 0-87322-785-9 • $14.95 ($20.95 Canadian)

Presents 15 fun activities to help K-12 students build self-confidence and improve interpersonal relationships, promote teamwork, and initiate problem-solving methods.

Team Building Through Physical Challenges
Donald R. Glover, MS, and Daniel W. Midura, MEd
1992 • Paper • 160 pp • Item BGLO0359
ISBN 0-87322-359-4 • $16.95 ($23.95 Canadian)

Features 22 Outward Bound-type tasks that challenge students to learn teamwork, practice leadership skills, improve listening skills, and appreciate individual differences.

Cooperative Learning in Physical Education
Steven Grineski, EdD
1996 • Paper • 152 pp • Item BGRI0879
ISBN 0-87322-879-0 • $15.00 ($22.50 Canadian)

Helps readers teach students to value each other through positive interdependence, individual accountability, and collaborative skills.

Multicultural Games
Lorraine Barbarash
1997 • Paper • 152 pp • Item BBAR0565
ISBN 0-88011-565-3 • $14.95 ($21.95 Canadian)

Provides 75 games from 43 countries or cultures on 6 continents to help students develop an awareness of and appreciation for other cultures while enjoying physical activity. Can help educators meet NASPE's national content standards for multicultural awareness at the elementary and middle school level.

Teaching Children Games
Becoming a Master Teacher

David E. Belka, PhD
1994 • Paper • 144 pp • Item BBEL0481
ISBN 0-87322-481-7 • $16.00 ($23.95 Canadian)

Includes 23 practical, child-tested game activities designed primarily for grades 3 through 6. Divided into five categories: tag, target, net and wall, invasion, and fielding.

To request more information or to order, U.S. customers call 1-800-747-4457, e-mail us at humank@hkusa.com, or visit our Web site at http://www.humankinetics.com/. Persons outside the U.S. can contact us via our Web site or use the appropriate telephone number, postal address, or e-mail address shown in the front of this book.

Human Kinetics
The Information Leader in Physical Activity

DATE DUE

MAR 0 3 2002

GAYLORD   PRINTED IN U.S.A.